MW01681061

Vital Leadership

Vital Leadership

Crafting Healthy Work Environments

Mackens Salomon

Mackens Salomon
Vital Leadership
Crafting Healthy Work Environments

All rights reserved
Copyright © 2025 by **Mackens Salomon**

No part of this publication may be reproduced, distributed, or transmitted in any form or by any means, including photocopying, recording, or other electronic or mechanical methods, without the prior written permission of the publisher, except in the case of brief quotations embodied in critical reviews and certain other noncommercial uses permitted by copyright law.

Disclaimer

The content provided in this book is intended for educational and informational purposes only. It is not designed to be a substitute for professional advice, whether legal, medical, or clinical. Readers are encouraged to seek the assistance of qualified professionals for specific concerns or situations. The author and publisher are not liable for any consequences.

Published by Spines Publishing Platform
ISBN: 979-8-90222-855-4

Spines

Contents

Front Matter

To every leader who has ever doubted their capacity to lead with heart, to all senior leaders, managers, and HR professionals striving to build more humane workplaces, and to all employees who have navigated the often-turbulent waters of professional life while carrying the silent weight of unseen struggles. This book is a testament to the profound impact that authentic, empathetic leadership can have, not just on individual lives, but on the very fabric of organizations. It is for those who believe that success should not come at the expense of well-being, and that a thriving business and a healthy workforce are not mutually exclusive goals, but rather intrinsically linked pillars of sustainable prosperity. May this guide serve as a beacon, illuminating the path toward workplaces where every individual feels seen, heard, and valued, fostering an environment where both people and performance can flourish. This work is dedicated to the brave souls who champion these ideals, often against prevailing norms, and who understand that true strength lies not in rigid control, but in compassionate connection and unwavering support for their teams. It is a tribute to the human spirit and its resilience when nurtured by a culture of psychological safety and genuine care.

The modern workplace is at a crossroads. While technological advancements and market demands continue to accelerate, a critical element often lags: our understanding and application of leadership that truly supports human flourishing. We are witnessing an unprecedented awareness of mental health challenges, not as isolated individual issues, but as deeply intertwined with the dynamics of our professional lives. Burnout, stress, and disengagement are no longer abstract concepts; they are palpable realities impacting productivity, innovation, and the fundamental well-being of our teams.

This book emerges from a conviction that leadership is not merely about achieving targets or managing resources but about cultivating environments where people can thrive. It is a response to the urgent need for a new paradigm of leadership —one that prioritizes psychological safety, embraces empathy as a strategic imperative, and understands the profound link between employee well-being and organizational success. The insights presented here are born from years of experience in organizational psychology, leadership development, and mental health advocacy, distilled into practical, actionable strategies.

We aim to equip leaders at all levels—from the C-suite to the front lines—and HR professionals with the tools and frameworks necessary to foster genuinely supportive workplaces. This is not about implementing a quick fix or a superficial wellness program; it is about fundamentally transforming the way we lead, interact, and build our organizations. It is about creating a culture where vulnerability is seen as strength, where open communication is encouraged, and where human experience is at the core of every decision.

Throughout these pages, we will explore the foundational principles of 'True Leadership,' delving into the practical, daily habits that build trust, foster resilience, and drive sustainable performance. We will provide concrete examples, data-driven insights, and policy considerations that demonstrate the tangible return on investment for prioritizing employee mental health. I hope that this book serves not just as a guide, but as a catalyst for change, empowering you to lead with greater intention, deeper connection, and a profound commitment to the well-being of your people. The journey toward creating truly humane and high-performing workplaces begins with a courageous embrace of empathy and a dedication to fostering environments where everyone can truly flourish.

In an era defined by rapid change and complex challenges, the landscape of leadership has undergone a significant evolution. The command-and-control models of the past, once the bedrock of corporate structure, are increasingly giving way to a more nuanced and human-centric approach. This shift is not merely a trend; it is a fundamental necessity driven by a growing understanding of the inextricable link between employee well-being and organizational success. We are no longer simply managing resources; we are leading people, and the caliber of leadership is directly reflected in the health, engagement, and performance of our teams.

This book, "The Wellbeing Advantage: Leadership Strategies for a Healthier Work Culture," is born from a deep-seated belief that effective leadership in the 21st century must be grounded in empathy, authenticity, and a proactive commitment to fostering psychological safety. It is for the leaders, HR professionals, and organizational development specialists who recognize that a thriving organization is built on the well-being of its people. You are likely at the forefront of shaping workplace culture, responsible for employee engagement, and seeking practical, evidence-based strategies to address escalating rates of stress, burnout, and disengagement.

We are living in a time where the conversation around mental health has moved from the fringes to the center stage. Employees are increasingly seeking workplaces that not only offer professional growth and fair compensation but also provide a supportive and understanding environment where their mental and emotional well-being is genuinely prioritized. This is no longer a 'nice-to-have'; it is a strategic imperative for attracting and retaining top talent, driving innovation, and ensuring long-term organizational resilience.

The pages that follow will guide you through the core principles of 'True Leadership,' a framework that emphasizes the foundational role of leaders in creating environments where individuals feel safe to be themselves, to take interpersonal risks, and to contribute their best without fear of reprisal. We will explore how cultivating psychological safety is not a soft skill but a critical determinant of team effectiveness. You will discover actionable daily habits that foster deeper connections, build trust, and proactively manage workloads to prevent burnout. Furthermore, we will delve into practical tools, policy frameworks, and data-driven approaches that empower you to measure success and embed a culture of care into the very DNA of your organization.

This book is designed to be your practical companion, offering relatable scenarios, clear guidance, and the robust evidence needed to make a compelling case for investing in employee well-being. It is a call to action for leaders to embrace their role as architects of positive, supportive, and high-performing workplaces, where both individuals and the organization can achieve their fullest potential. Let us embark on this essential journey together, transforming our workplaces into beacons of support, growth, and enduring success.

Chapter 1
The Evolution of Leadership

The landscape of leadership is undergoing a profound transformation. For decades, the prevailing model often resembled a hierarchical pyramid, a structure where authority flowed from the top down, and success was primarily measured by adherence to directives and quantifiable outputs. This traditional "command-and-control" paradigm, while effective in certain industrial contexts, frequently prioritized efficiency and obedience over the nuanced human experience of employees. Leaders in this era were often seen as the ultimate arbiters of knowledge, expected to provide all the answers, maintain an unassailable demeanor, and drive results through direct instruction and, at times, implicit threat of consequence. The focus was on managing tasks, processes, and resources, with the individual employee often viewed as a cog in a larger machine, whose personal well-being was secondary to the operational needs of the organization. This approach, while it could yield short-term gains, often did so at the expense of long-term employee engagement, innovation, and crucially, mental health. The underlying assumption was that emotional detachment and a focus solely on productivity were the hallmarks of strong leadership.

However, the modern workplace is a vastly different ecosystem. It is characterized by rapid technological advancements, shifting economic landscapes, and a workforce that increasingly values purpose, connection, and well-being. In this dynamic environment, the command-and-control model is proving to be not only outdated but also detrimental. The consequences of leadership that neglects the human element are becoming increasingly apparent: higher rates of burnout, disengagement, employee turnover, and a pervasive sense of anxiety and stress that can permeate an entire organization. Employees are no longer content to follow orders simply; they seek to be part of something meaningful, to feel valued for their contributions, and to work in an environment that supports their holistic well-being. This shift in employee expectations, coupled with a growing body of research highlighting the inextricable link between psychological safety and organizational performance, has given rise to a new, more effective, and fundamentally human-centric leadership framework: "True Leadership."

True Leadership is not merely a buzzword or a fleeting trend; it represents a fundamental evolution in how we understand and practice leadership in the 21st century. At its core, True Leadership is characterized by authenticity, empathy, transparency, and a genuine, demonstrable concern for the well-being of every individual on the team. It moves beyond the transactional nature of traditional leadership to foster deep, trusting relationships built on mutual respect and understanding. This is not about being "soft" or compromising on accountability; rather, it is about recognizing that human beings are not simply resources to be managed, but individuals with unique needs, aspirations, and vulnerabilities. Leaders who embrace this approach understand that fostering a psychologically safe environment—one where people feel secure to be themselves, to take interpersonal risks, and to voice their thoughts and concerns without fear of negative repercussions—is not a discretionary perk, but a strategic imperative.

Authenticity is a cornerstone of True Leadership. It means leaders are genuine in their interactions, aligning their words with their actions. They are not afraid to be human, to acknowledge their own limitations, and to learn from their mistakes. This vulnerability, when shared appropriately, builds bridges of trust and encourages others to be equally open. Transparency is another critical pillar. True Leaders are open about organizational goals, challenges, and decisions, providing context and clarity that helps employees understand the bigger picture and their role within it. This openness reduces speculation, builds confidence, and fosters a sense of shared ownership. When employees feel they are being kept in the loop, they are more likely to feel valued and respected, leading to greater commitment and engagement.

However, perhaps the most defining characteristic of True Leadership in the modern workplace is profound and actionable empathy.

Empathy, in this context, goes far beyond simply acknowledging someone's feelings; it involves actively seeking to understand their perspective, their experiences, and their emotional state. It means stepping into their shoes, even if only for a moment, to grasp the impact of decisions, events, or workloads on their well-being. This empathetic understanding allows leaders to tailor their support, address concerns proactively, and make decisions that are not only effective from a business perspective but also humane and considerate of the people carrying out the work. It is this genuine concern for employee well-being, demonstrated consistently through words and deeds, that truly distinguishes True Leadership from its predecessors.

The shift to True Leadership is not simply about adopting a new set of behaviors; it is about a fundamental reorientation of leadership philosophy. It recognizes that the most valuable asset any organization possesses is its people, and that their mental and emotional well-being is directly correlated with their ability to perform, innovate, and contribute to collective success. Leaders who prioritize the human element of their teams are, in essence, investing in the long-term health and resilience of their organization. They are cultivating environments where trust flourishes, where open communication is the norm, and where individuals feel empowered to bring their whole selves to work. This foundational understanding is crucial because it sets the stage for the subsequent discussions on the specific behaviors, tools, and strategies that enable leaders not only to define but also to embody True Leadership and, in doing so, foster environments where mental health is not just acknowledged but actively supported and prioritized.

The traditional leadership playbook, often characterized by a "what gets measured gets managed" mentality, frequently overlooks the intangible yet critical factors that contribute to a thriving workforce. In this older model, leadership success was often equated with an unyielding focus on key performance indicators (KPIs) related to output, deadlines, and profit margins. The human element, including the psychological state of employees, was largely relegated to the background, considered a secondary concern or even an individual responsibility outside the purview of managerial duty. Leaders were trained to be decisive, objective, and, in many cases, emotionally detached, believing that vulnerability or deep concern for personal issues would undermine their authority. The prevailing narrative suggested that professional success necessitated a certain level of stoicism, where personal struggles were to be compartmentalized and left at the doorstep of the workplace. This approach, while seemingly efficient on the surface, created environments where employees often felt pressure to mask their true feelings, leading to increased stress, anxiety, and a pervasive sense of isolation. The focus on individual achievement, often at the expense of collective well-being, fostered a competitive rather than collaborative spirit, where speaking up about difficulties or admitting mistakes could be perceived as weakness.

The repercussions of this approach were often subtle yet insidious, manifesting as a gradual erosion of morale, a decline in innovation, and a heightened risk of burnout. Leaders operating under the command-and-control paradigm might have seen rising productivity metrics as a sign of success, failing to recognize the underlying costs being incurred in terms of employee mental and emotional health. This created a fragile success, one that was susceptible to collapse when the human toll became unsustainable. The very systems designed to drive performance often inadvertently suppress the very qualities that foster long-term organizational resilience: creativity, collaboration, and a willingness to take intelligent risks. The emphasis on strict adherence to process, while important, often leaves little room for adaptability and innovative thinking that emerge when individuals feel psychologically secure and are encouraged to share diverse perspectives.

In contrast, the emerging framework of "True Leadership" fundamentally challenges these outdated notions. It posits that a leader's primary responsibility extends beyond mere task management to encompass the cultivation of an environment where individuals can flourish both professionally and personally. This paradigm shift is rooted in the understanding that employee well-being, particularly mental health, is not a separate or secondary concern, but an intrinsic component of overall organizational performance.

True Leaders recognize that the human mind and emotions are not merely variables to be controlled, but integral forces that drive *productivity, creativity, and commitment.* Therefore, fostering positive mental health is not a philanthropic gesture; it is a strategic investment in the organization's most valuable resource.

This new understanding necessitates a redefinition of leadership itself. True Leadership is characterized by authenticity, empathy, and transparency. Authenticity means leaders are genuine, their actions align with their words, and their values are evident in their behavior. They are willing to be human, to acknowledge their own fallibilities, and to learn from their experiences, creating a space where others feel safe to do the same.

Transparency involves open communication about goals, challenges, and decisions, providing context and fostering a sense of shared purpose and trust. When employees understand the 'why' behind the 'what,' they are more likely to be engaged and to contribute their best efforts.

At the heart of True Leadership lies empathy – the ability to understand and share the feelings of others. This is not a passive sentiment but an active practice. Empathetic leaders make a conscious effort to see situations from their team members' perspectives, to acknowledge their challenges, and to offer support tailored to their individual needs. This empathetic approach builds strong relationships, fosters trust, and creates a sense of psychological safety.

Psychological safety is the bedrock upon which high-performing teams are built. It is the shared belief that the team is safe for *interpersonal risk-taking*, meaning individuals feel comfortable speaking up, asking questions, admitting mistakes, and offering new ideas without fear of embarrassment or punishment. Leaders who champion empathy are the architects of this safety. They create a culture where vulnerability is not seen as a weakness but as a strength, where open dialogue is encouraged across all levels, and where individuals feel valued and respected for their unique contributions.

The implications of this shift are profound. Leaders who prioritize the human element are not just creating more pleasant workplaces; they are building more resilient, innovative, and productive organizations. They understand that by investing in the mental and emotional well-being of their teams, they unlock the full potential of their workforce. This foundational understanding is critical because it moves the conversation beyond abstract ideals to concrete strategic advantages. It sets the stage for delving into the specific behaviors and practices that leaders can adopt to cultivate psychological safety and, by extension, to drive superior organizational outcomes. This new definition of leadership is not about sacrificing results for well-being; it is about recognizing that true, sustainable success is achieved when both are prioritized and integrated. It's a move from managing people as cogs to leading them as complex, capable individuals, unlocking a richer, more productive, and more humane way of working.

The traditional organizational structures and leadership philosophies that once dominated the professional landscape are increasingly being recognized as inadequate for the complexities of the modern world. For a significant period, leadership was often synonymous with authority, control, and a detached, objective approach to management. This model, often referred to as "command-and-control," emphasized hierarchy, strict adherence to protocols, and a clear delineation of power and responsibility. Leaders were expected to be the repositories of all knowledge, the ultimate decision-makers, and the driving force behind every initiative. Their role was to direct, monitor, and ensure compliance, with the individual employee often viewed as a resource to be deployed efficiently rather than a multifaceted human being with unique needs and aspirations. Success was primarily measured by quantifiable outcomes: deadlines met, quotas achieved, and profits maximized. The emotional or psychological state of the workforce was, at best, a secondary consideration, often viewed as an individual concern rather than a collective responsibility for leadership. This approach, while capable of driving output in stable environments, often inadvertently stifles creativity, discourages open communication, and creates a breeding ground for stress, anxiety, and ultimately, burnout.

The repercussions of this traditional leadership model are becoming increasingly evident in today's workplace. The constant pressure to perform, coupled with a perceived lack of genuine support or understanding from leadership, can lead to a disengagement that goes beyond mere dissatisfaction. Employees may become less likely to share innovative ideas, to admit mistakes, or to speak up about potential issues, fearing negative repercussions. This suppression of authentic expression can lead to a culture of conformity, where risk-taking is discouraged, and the organization becomes less agile and less adaptable to change. Furthermore, the emotional toll on individuals can be significant, contributing to higher rates of absenteeism, presenteeism (being physically present but mentally disengaged), and employee turnover. The cost of replacing employees, both in terms of recruitment and lost productivity, is substantial, and a direct consequence of a leadership style that fails to nurture its human capital.

In response to these challenges, a new paradigm for leadership has emerged, one that is proving to be far more effective in fostering both employee well-being and organizational success. This evolving framework, which we can term "True Leadership," shifts the focus from control and command to connection and care. It recognizes that the most impactful leaders are those who prioritize the human element of their teams, creating environments where individuals feel valued, respected, and psychologically safe. This is not a capitulation to softer approaches; rather, it is a strategic recognition that genuine human connection and a deep understanding of employee needs are the drivers of sustainable high performance.

Chapter 2
Cultivating Authenticity, Empathy, and Psychological Safety in True Leadership

At the heart of True Leadership lies a commitment to authenticity. This means leaders are genuine in their interactions, their actions aligning with their stated values. They are willing to be vulnerable, to admit when they don't have all the answers, and to learn from their mistakes. This authenticity builds trust and encourages others to be equally open. Transparency is another crucial tenet. True Leaders are open about organizational goals, challenges, and decision-making processes, providing context and clarity that helps employees understand their role in the bigger picture. This open communication reduces uncertainty, fosters a sense of shared purpose, and builds confidence in leadership.

However, the most distinctive characteristic of True Leadership is its profound emphasis on empathy. Empathy, in this context, is not simply about sympathizing with someone's plight; it is about actively seeking to understand their perspective, their experiences, and their emotional state. Empathetic leaders make a conscious effort to listen, to ask clarifying questions, and to acknowledge the impact of events or decisions on their team members. This empathetic approach is the bedrock upon which psychological safety is built. Psychological safety is the shared belief that the team is safe for interpersonal risk-taking. It is an environment where individuals feel comfortable speaking up, asking questions, admitting errors, and proposing new ideas without fear of humiliation, punishment, or judgment.

Leaders who embody True Leadership are the primary architects of this psychologically safe environment. They understand that by creating a space where vulnerability is embraced and open dialogue is encouraged, they foster an atmosphere of trust and mutual respect. This trust is essential for collaboration, innovation, and problem-solving. When employees feel safe to express themselves, they are more likely to contribute their unique insights, challenge the status quo constructively, and work collaboratively towards shared goals. This human-centric approach to leadership is not merely a "nice-to-have"; it is a strategic imperative for any organization seeking to thrive in the modern business landscape. By prioritizing the well-being and psychological safety of their teams, True Leaders cultivate an environment where individuals can perform at their best, leading to enhanced engagement, increased productivity, and greater overall organizational resilience. This foundational understanding sets the stage for exploring the specific behaviors and practices that enable leaders to translate these principles into tangible, positive impacts on their teams and the organization. The journey towards True Leadership begins with this fundamental shift in perspective—recognizing that people, in all their complexity, are the ultimate drivers of success.

The notion that an organization's bottom line is solely determined by financial acumen, market positioning, or technological innovation is a relic of a bygone era. In the contemporary business environment, a more profound and indispensable link has emerged, one that underpins sustained success and competitive advantage: the inextricable connection between the mental well-being of employees and overall organizational performance. This correlation is not a matter of anecdotal observation or a "soft" HR initiative; it is a quantifiable reality supported by robust research and tangible economic impact studies. Leaders who fail to recognize and actively nurture the psychological health of their workforce are, in essence, overlooking a critical driver of productivity, innovation, and long-term resilience.

The evidence unequivocally demonstrates that environments prioritizing mental well-being foster demonstrably higher levels of productivity. When employees feel supported, less stressed, and psychologically safe, their cognitive functions are optimized. They are more focused, more engaged, and better equipped to handle complex tasks. Studies by organizations like the World Health Organization (WHO) and numerous academic institutions have consistently shown that mentally healthy employees exhibit higher levels of concentration, better problem-solving capabilities, and a greater capacity for sustained effort. Conversely, workplaces characterized by high levels of stress, anxiety, and a lack of support contribute to a significant decline in cognitive performance. Employees struggling with mental health challenges often experience difficulties with memory, decision-making, and attention span, directly impacting their output and the quality of their work. This translates into tangible financial losses for organizations through reduced efficiency and increased errors.

Beyond individual productivity, the link between mental well-being and innovation is equally compelling. Innovation thrives in an atmosphere of psychological safety, where individuals feel empowered to share novel ideas, experiment without fear of reprisal, and engage in constructive debate. When employees are burdened by anxiety or fear of judgment, their willingness to take creative risks diminishes significantly. They may self-censor, opting for the status quo rather than risking potential criticism. Conversely, organizations that cultivate positive mental health environments, characterized by open communication, supportive feedback, and a tolerance for failure as a learning opportunity, witness a surge in creativity and innovation. This leads to the development of new products, services, and more efficient processes, providing a crucial competitive edge in dynamic markets. Research into corporate innovation often highlights a culture of trust and psychological safety as a prerequisite for breakthrough thinking.

Employee retention is another critical area profoundly influenced by mental well-being. High turnover rates are a significant drain on organizational resources, encompassing recruitment costs, training expenses, and the loss of institutional knowledge and productivity. The primary drivers of employee dissatisfaction and subsequent departure are often rooted in workplace stressors, lack of support, and a feeling of being undervalued or overwhelmed. Organizations that invest in mental health support systems, promote work-life balance, and foster a culture of care are far more likely to retain their talented employees. A 2020 Deloitte report, for instance, indicated that for every $1 invested in mental health initiatives, organizations see a return of $4 in increased productivity and reduced absenteeism and turnover. This economic argument is powerful: retaining skilled individuals who are mentally healthy is significantly more cost-effective than the perpetual cycle of recruitment and onboarding driven by a toxic or unsupportive work environment.

The economic toll of poor mental well-being manifests acutely through absenteeism and presenteeism. Absenteeism, the simple act of not showing up to work, is a direct financial cost. Employees experiencing mental health issues are more likely to take sick days. However, the subtler, and often more damaging, cost is presenteeism. This refers to the phenomenon of employees coming to work while not fully functioning due to illness or mental distress. While they are physically present, their productivity is severely compromised. They may take longer to complete tasks, make more mistakes, and interact less effectively with colleagues. The economic impact of presenteeism, as estimated by various studies, can far outweigh that of absenteeism. For example, research cited by the American Psychiatric Association suggests that presenteeism due to depression alone costs U.S. businesses billions of dollars annually in lost productivity. Addressing mental health is therefore not just about employee welfare; it's about safeguarding operational efficiency and financial viability.

The financial implications of neglecting mental health are stark and quantifiable. Beyond the direct costs of absenteeism and presenteeism, organizations face indirect costs related to decreased morale, damaged reputation, and potential legal liabilities if workplace conditions contribute to mental distress. A proactive approach, however, yields significant returns.

Investing in comprehensive mental health programs, including access to counseling services, stress management workshops, mindfulness training, and leadership development focused on empathetic management, is not an expense but a strategic investment. These investments cultivate a more engaged, productive, and loyal workforce, leading to enhanced customer satisfaction, improved brand perception, and ultimately, sustained profitability. The economic case for prioritizing mental well-being is clear: it is a fundamental component of a robust and resilient business strategy.

Consider a hypothetical scenario, although grounded in common organizational experiences. Imagine a technology firm where project deadlines are consistently aggressive, and the leadership culture, inherited from more traditional eras, emphasizes long hours and a "hustle" mentality. Employees frequently work late into the night; their personal lives are often encroached upon by urgent requests and the implicit pressure to be constantly available. In such an environment, stress and anxiety become pervasive. Team members may have trouble concentrating during critical brainstorming sessions, their creativity stifled by the underlying tension. Mistakes, though minor individually, begin to accumulate across projects, leading to delays and increased rework. Absenteeism might tick up slightly, but the more insidious impact is presenteeism: employees drag themselves to work, exhausted and mentally drained, their capacity for deep thinking and problem-solving severely diminished. They might sit in meetings, nodding along but unable to fully engage or contribute their best ideas.

The consequences for this firm are multifaceted. Productivity suffers as tasks take longer to complete. Innovation stagnates;

the challenging deadlines leave no room for exploration or experimentation, and employees are too fatigued to think outside the box. The company culture becomes one of quiet desperation rather than collaborative problem-solving. As a result, key engineers, feeling burnt out and unsupported, begin to look elsewhere for opportunities where their well-being is prioritized. The recruitment pipeline, while active, struggles to replace the nuanced skills and institutional knowledge of those who leave. The cost of replacing each departing employee through recruitment fees, onboarding, and lost productivity during the transition is substantial, running into tens of thousands of dollars per individual. Furthermore, the firm's reputation among potential hires might begin to suffer, making it harder to attract top talent in the future. The cumulative effect of these factors, including reduced productivity, stifled innovation, high turnover, and increased operational costs, directly impacts the company's financial performance and its ability to compete effectively.

Now, in contrast with a similar technology firm, let's call "InnovateTech," which has consciously adopted a leadership philosophy that prioritizes mental well-being. InnovateTech's leaders understand the business imperative of supporting their employees. They have implemented several key initiatives. Firstly, they have invested in mental health resources, offering employees confidential access to therapy, counseling services, and mental wellness apps. Secondly, they have trained their managers to recognize the signs of burnout and stress, equipping them with the skills to have supportive conversations and offer flexible work arrangements where possible. Thirdly, they have re-evaluated project management methodologies, ensuring that deadlines are ambitious but realistic, and that workloads are distributed equitably, encouraging a healthy work-life balance. They actively promote a culture where it's acceptable to take breaks, disconnect after work hours, and seek support when needed.

The impact on InnovateTech is palpable. Employees, feeling valued and supported, exhibit higher levels of engagement and focus. Their cognitive functions are sharp, enabling them to tackle complex coding challenges and design innovative solutions. During team meetings, there is a vibrant exchange of ideas, with individuals confidently proposing new approaches and offering constructive feedback, knowing they will not be penalized for challenging the norm. Absenteeism is low, and presenteeism is significantly reduced because employees feel well enough to perform at their peak. When minor setbacks occur, the team rallies together, supporting each other and problem-solving collaboratively, rather than succumbing to stress or blame.

The economic benefits for InnovateTech are substantial. Productivity is consistently high, with projects delivered on time and to a high standard, often ahead of schedule due to efficient problem-solving. Innovation flourishes: the company releases novel features and products at a competitive pace, capturing market share and enhancing its brand. Employee retention rates are exceptionally high. Talented individuals are loyal to a company that genuinely cares for their well-being, reducing recruitment and training costs dramatically. Furthermore, the positive work environment attracts top talent, creating a virtuous cycle of high performance and continuous improvement. Industry analysts note InnovateTech's strong culture and consistent delivery, contributing to a positive market perception and increased investor confidence. The return on investment in mental health initiatives is not just evident in employee satisfaction scores. Still, it is directly reflected in the company's robust financial performance, its agility in the market, and its long-term sustainability. This stark comparison underscores that mental well-being is not a discretionary add-on; it is a fundamental driver of organizational success.

The imperative for leaders to understand and act upon this connection is therefore not merely ethical; it is a strategic necessity. Failing to invest in the mental well-being of the workforce is, by definition, an act of underinvestment in the core engine of the organization. The data is overwhelming: from increased productivity and enhanced innovation to improved employee retention and reduced operational costs, the positive impact of a mentally healthy workforce is undeniable. Leaders who embrace this truth and embed it into their organizational culture and practices are not only building better workplaces but are also building more successful, resilient, and future-ready businesses. The business case is clear, compelling, and increasingly difficult to ignore in a world where human capital is the ultimate differentiator.

Psychological safety, at its core, is the bedrock upon which truly thriving teams are built. It's not a fluffy concept relegated to HR jargon; it's a tangible, shared belief within a team that it is safe for interpersonal risk-taking. This means individuals feel confident that they can speak up with ideas, questions, concerns, or even admit mistakes, without facing undue embarrassment, punishment, or a threat to their professional standing. It is the understanding that within this group, vulnerability is not a weakness to be exploited, but a natural human experience that is met with respect and understanding. When this safety is present, teams unlock their full potential, fostering innovation, enhancing problem-solving, and ultimately achieving higher levels of performance. Conversely, a lack of psychological safety creates an environment of apprehension, where individuals self-censor, avoid risks, and operate from a place of fear rather than engagement.

Leaders are the primary architects of this crucial environment. Their words, actions, and the very culture they cultivate are the building blocks that either construct a fortress of safety or a breeding ground for anxiety. The behaviors leaders exhibit can either reinforce this shared belief or systematically dismantle it, often unintentionally. For instance, a leader who consistently dismisses or belittles suggestions that deviate from their own thinking, or who publicly reprimands an employee for a minor error, is inadvertently signaling that speaking up or making mistakes is a perilous endeavor. This creates a chilling effect, where others become hesitant to share their nascent ideas or admit to fumbling a task, fearing a similar public display of disapproval.

Conversely, leaders who actively solicit diverse opinions, even when those opinions are critical or unconventional, lay a strong foundation for psychological safety. When a leader visibly listens, asks clarifying questions, and thanks individuals for their contributions, regardless of whether their idea is adopted, they send a powerful message: "Your voice matters, and your perspective is valued." Similarly, when a leader openly admits their own mistakes, discusses challenges they faced, and frames failures as learning opportunities, they normalize vulnerability. This act of self-disclosure can be incredibly disarming and empowering for team members, creating an atmosphere where admitting one's own fallibility is seen not as a sign of incompetence, but as a human trait that fosters connection and learning.

Consider the contrast between two leaders managing project teams facing unexpected technical hurdles. Leader A, when a critical component fails, immediately calls a team meeting and demands to know who is responsible, his tone accusatory. He might point fingers, express frustration openly, and declare that this oversight is unacceptable. The team members, feeling the palpable tension and sensing the danger, might offer vague explanations or try to deflect blame, even if they know the root cause. Some might even withhold information they believe could indirectly implicate them, further obscuring the real issue. The focus shifts from problem-solving to self-preservation. In this scenario, psychological safety is severely eroded. The next time a similar challenge arises, team members will be far less likely to proactively report the problem or admit they are struggling, fearing the leader's predictable wrath.

Leader B, faced with the same technical failure, adopts a different approach. She convinces the team and begins by acknowledging the setback: "This is a significant challenge, and it's clearly impacting our progress. Let's figure out what happened and how we can fix it together." She might then ask, "From what you saw, what do you think led to this issue?" She actively listens to each person's input, encouraging them to share their observations and analyses. If an individual admits they missed a crucial step, Leader B might respond with, "Thanks for being upfront about that. We all make mistakes, and your honesty helps us understand the situation. What can we learn from this to ensure it doesn't happen again?" She might also share a similar experience from her own career, demonstrating that mistakes are part of the learning process. In this environment, team members feel safe to admit their role in the problem, to ask for help, and to discuss potential solutions openly. Psychological safety is fostered, enabling the team to address the issue effectively and learn from the experience.

The leader's role in encouraging open dialogue extends beyond crisis management. It's about creating consistent opportunities for team members to voice their thoughts and concerns. This can be achieved through various mechanisms, such as regular one-on-one meetings where open-ended questions are prioritized ("What's on your mind?" "What challenges are you facing that I might not be aware of?"), team meetings that explicitly allocate time for questions and feedback, or through anonymous feedback channels that, when used effectively, can provide valuable insights without individual risk. The key is to demonstrate a genuine interest in hearing from everyone, and crucially, to act upon the feedback received. Ignoring feedback or responding with defensiveness will quickly shut down any avenue for open communication.

Embracing vulnerability as a leadership trait is paramount. This doesn't mean oversharing or displaying emotional instability, but rather demonstrating a willingness to be human. When leaders share their own learning curves, their moments of uncertainty, or acknowledge that they don't have all the answers, they create space for others to do the same. This can be as simple as saying, "I'm not entirely sure about the best way forward on this. I'd love to hear your thoughts." Or "I tried something similar in the past, and it didn't quite work out as planned. Here's what I learned." These authentic moments of self-disclosure build trust and make it easier for team members to admit their own perceived shortcomings without fear of judgment.

Furthermore, leaders must be vigilant about the implicit messages they send. The tone of voice, body language, and even the physical environment can contribute to or detract from psychological safety. A leader who is perpetually rushed, constantly checking their phone during conversations, or whose facial expressions convey impatience sends a clear signal that their team members' input is not their top priority. Conversely, a leader who makes eye contact, listens attentively, and creates a welcoming space for discussion demonstrates respect and signals that the interaction is valued. This attention to the subtle nuances of communication is vital for building and maintaining a safe environment.

Chapter 3
The Power of Psychological Safety

The impact of psychological safety reverberates across all aspects of team performance. When individuals feel safe, they are more likely to engage in "voice behavior"—the act of speaking up with suggestions, concerns, or creative ideas. Research consistently shows a strong correlation between psychological safety and voice behavior, which in turn drives innovation and problem-solving. Team members are not afraid to challenge the status quo, propose novel solutions, or point out potential flaws in a plan, knowing their contributions will be considered, not condemned. This open exchange of ideas fuels creativity and leads to more robust decision-making.

Consider a team developing a new software product. In a psychologically safe environment, a junior developer might feel empowered to question a design choice made by a senior architect, not out of defiance, but out of a genuine concern for user experience or technical feasibility. They might say,

"I've been thinking about this particular feature, and I'm concerned that the current approach might lead to performance issues under heavy load. I have an idea for an alternative that might be more scalable." In a non-safe environment, that junior developer might keep their concerns to themselves, fearing they'd be dismissed as inexperienced or that they'd be seen as challenging authority. This silence could lead to a critical flaw being embedded in the product, only to be discovered much later at a greater cost to fix.

Admitting mistakes is another critical component of psychological safety. When leaders create an environment where errors are treated as learning opportunities rather than grounds for punishment, team members are more likely to be transparent about their slip-ups. This transparency is invaluable for identifying systemic issues, improving processes, and preventing future errors. A team that can openly discuss what went wrong, without fear of retribution, can quickly course-correct and learn collectively. This fosters a culture of continuous improvement, where the focus is on growth and development rather than blame.

In contrast, a *blame-oriented culture* breeds a fear of accountability. When mistakes are met with harsh criticism, disciplinary action, or public shaming, individuals will do whatever it takes to avoid admitting their errors. This can lead to a cascade of negative consequences: problems festering unaddressed, crucial information being withheld, and a general reluctance to take on challenging tasks for fear of failure. The team's ability to learn and adapt is severely hampered, leading to stagnation and decreased overall effectiveness.

Leaders also play a crucial role in ensuring that everyone's voice is heard, not just the loudest or most dominant personalities. This involves actively drawing out quieter members of the team, creating structured opportunities for participation, and ensuring that discussions remain respectful and inclusive. Techniques such as round-robin sharing of ideas, using anonymous polling for sensitive topics, or actively calling on individuals who haven't yet spoken can help to level the playing field and ensure that a diversity of perspectives is captured. It’s about creating a space where introverts feel as comfortable contributing as extroverts, and where junior members feel as empowered to speak as senior ones.

The concept of "interpersonal risk-taking" is central to psychological safety. This encompasses a range of behaviors, from asking seemingly "dumb" questions and admitting uncertainty to offering constructive criticism and proposing unconventional ideas. In a psychologically safe team, these actions are not viewed as liabilities but as essential contributions to collective learning and problem-solving. A leader’s response to these actions is critical. A leader who patiently answers questions, even those that seem basic, validates the inquirer's need for clarity. A leader who encourages debate and discussion, even when it challenges their own viewpoints, demonstrates an openness to different perspectives.

Consider the act of asking for help. In many traditional hierarchical structures, asking for help can be perceived as a sign of weakness or incompetence. Employees might struggle in silence, trying to solve a problem on their own, even if it means falling behind or producing subpar work, because they fear being judged as incapable. However, in a team with high psychological safety, asking for help is a sign of strength and a commitment to the team's success. It signals that the individual values the team's collective intelligence and is willing to leverage it to overcome obstacles. Leaders can foster this by normalizing the act of seeking assistance. When a leader openly asks for help from their team, or when they publicly acknowledge the assistance they received from others, they set a powerful example.

Furthermore, the impact of psychological safety extends to conflict resolution. In teams where it is absent, disagreements often escalate into personal attacks or are avoided altogether, leading to unresolved tensions. In contrast, teams with high psychological safety can navigate conflict constructively. They can disagree on ideas without attacking individuals, express differing opinions respectfully, and work towards mutually acceptable solutions. This ability to manage conflict effectively allows teams to address challenges head-on and emerge with stronger, more considered outcomes. Leaders can facilitate this by setting clear ground rules for respectful dialogue, mediating disputes when necessary, and modeling constructive conflict resolution behaviors.

The leader's commitment to psychological safety must be unwavering and consistent. It cannot be a one-off initiative or a set of platitudes. It must be embedded in the daily interactions, the performance management systems, and the strategic decision-making processes of the organization. This means actively seeking feedback on the team's psychological safety, being open to constructive criticism about one's own leadership style and continuously iterating on practices to ensure that the environment remains safe and supportive.

Ultimately, psychological safety is not about eliminating risk or ensuring everyone always agrees. It is about creating an environment where people feel safe to take the necessary interpersonal risks that lead to innovation, learning, and high performance. It is about fostering a culture of trust, respect, and open communication, where every team member feels valued, heard, and empowered to contribute their best. Leaders who understand and actively cultivate psychological safety are not just building better teams; they are building organizations that are more resilient, adaptable, and ultimately, more successful in the long run. They are the architects of a workplace where human potential can truly flourish. This foundational element is critical because without it, even the most brilliant strategies or talented individuals will struggle to achieve their full potential, operating within the confines of fear and apprehension rather than the boundless possibilities of safety and trust. The ripple effect of this safety extends beyond individual teams, shaping the broader organizational culture and its capacity for sustained excellence. It is the intangible yet profoundly impactful force that separates teams that merely function from those that truly thrive.

Empathy, often relegated to the realm of "soft skills," is in fact a potent strategic tool, a critical leadership competency that underpins the very foundation of psychological safety. It's not about being overly sentimental or emotional but about possessing a profound capacity to understand and share the feelings of another and then translating that understanding into actionable behaviors. This ability to connect with your team on a human level is not a mere nicety; it's a deliberate and highly effective strategy for building trust, fostering collaboration, and ultimately, unlocking the full potential of every individual. Empathetic leaders don't just manage tasks; they nurture people, recognizing that the emotional landscape of the workplace directly impacts performance, innovation, and resilience.

Cultivating and demonstrating empathy requires moving beyond superficial acknowledgments. It's about a genuine commitment to understanding the perspectives, emotions, and experiences of your team members. This begins with mastering the art of active listening. Active listening is far more than simply hearing words; it involves fully concentrating, understanding, responding, and remembering what is being said, both verbally and non-verbally. When a team member is speaking, put away distractions – close your laptop, turn away from your monitor, and make direct eye contact. Resist the urge to formulate your response while they are still speaking. Instead, focus entirely on absorbing their message. Nodding, using brief verbal affirmations like "I see" or "Uh-huh," and mirroring their body language subtly can signal your engagement. More importantly, it's about listening to the underlying emotions and unstated concerns. A team member might say, "I'm a little worried about this deadline." But their tone, posture, and facial expression might convey a deeper sense of overwhelm or anxiety about their own capability. Your role as an empathetic leader is to pick up on these subtle cues.

Empathetic questioning is another crucial technique. Instead of asking closed-ended questions that elicit a simple "yes" or "no," opt for open-ended questions that encourage elaboration and deeper reflection. For instance, instead of asking, "Did you finish that report?" try, "How are you feeling about the progress of that report?" or "What are your thoughts on the approach we're taking for this project?" Questions like "Can you tell me more about what's making you feel that way?" or "What would be most helpful for you right now?" demonstrate a genuine interest in their experience and empower them to articulate their needs. These questions are invitations to share, creating a safe space for vulnerability. They signal that you are not just looking for a status update, but for a deeper understanding of their challenges and contributions.

The importance of acknowledging the emotional impact of workplace events cannot be overstated. Whether it's a project setback, a challenging client interaction, or a significant organizational change, these events carry an emotional weight. An empathetic leader doesn't ignore this reality. Instead, they validate these feelings. For example, after a difficult meeting where a team's proposal was rejected, an empathetic leader might say, "I understand that it's disappointing that our proposal wasn't accepted. We put a lot of work into it, and it's natural to feel frustrated. Let's take some time to debrief what we learned from the process." This acknowledgment validates the team's efforts and their emotional response, preventing them from feeling dismissed or unappreciated. It creates an environment where emotions are seen as a normal part of work experience, not something to be suppressed.

Consider a scenario where a project is significantly delayed due to unforeseen technical difficulties. A non-empathetic leader might focus solely on the missed deadline, demanding explanations and assigning blame. This approach, as we've seen, erodes psychological safety. An empathetic leader, however, would first acknowledge the team's hard work and the frustration of the setback. They might initiate a conversation by saying, "I know everyone has been working incredibly hard on this project, and this delay is a tough blow. It's completely understandable to feel frustrated and concerned right now. Let's talk about what happened, not to point fingers, but to understand the challenges we faced and how we can move forward constructively." This approach opens the door for a more honest and productive discussion. The leader could then follow up with empathetic questions: "What were the biggest hurdles you encountered?" or "What support do you feel you need to get back on track?" By acknowledging the emotional toll and facilitating a supportive problem-solving process, the leader strengthens the team's resilience and reinforces their trust.

Building stronger relationships is a direct outcome of empathetic leadership. When team members feel understood and valued, they are more likely to feel connected to their leader and to each other. This sense of belonging and trust is the bedrock of effective teamwork. Empathetic leaders create opportunities for informal connection, not just formal meetings. This could be a brief check-in at the start of a team meeting, a quick coffee chat, or even a shared experience outside of immediate project work. These interactions, however small, signal genuine care and interest in individuals beyond their professional output. They help to humanize the leader and the team, making it easier to navigate challenges together.

Furthermore, empathy is instrumental in effective conflict resolution. In any team, disagreements are inevitable. However, the way these disagreements are handled can either escalate into destructive conflict or transform into opportunities for growth and deeper understanding. Empathetic leaders approach conflict not as a threat, but as a signal that different perspectives need to be heard and understood. They facilitate conversations where all parties feel safe to express their views without fear of judgment or retribution. This often involves helping individuals to articulate their needs and concerns clearly and to listen to the other person's perspective with a genuine desire to understand.

Imagine a situation where two team members have conflicting ideas about the best strategy for a marketing campaign. A leader focused solely on achieving a predefined outcome might push for their own preferred approach or allow the loudest voice to dominate. An empathetic leader, however, would recognize the value in both perspectives. They would facilitate a discussion where each person can explain the rationale behind their approach, focusing on the 'why' rather than just the 'what'. The leader might ask questions like, "Sarah, can you elaborate on why you believe this approach will resonate most with our target audience?" and to the other team member, "John, what are your key concerns about Sarah's proposed strategy, and what outcomes do you believe your approach will achieve?" The leader would then help them to identify common ground and to explore potential hybrid solutions that incorporate the strengths of both ideas. This process not only resolves the immediate conflict but also teaches the team valuable lessons in collaborative problem-solving and respectful disagreement. It reinforces the idea that diverse viewpoints are not obstacles but assets.

Chapter 4

Empathy, Humility, and Accountability: The Cornerstones of Effective Leadership

The emotional intelligence of a leader is inextricably linked to their ability to demonstrate empathy. This involves self-awareness – understanding one's own emotions and how they might influence interactions – and social awareness – the ability to perceive and understand the emotions of others. For instance, a leader who is feeling stressed might be tempted to be curt or impatient. An emotionally intelligent and empathetic leader will recognize this internal state and consciously manage their behavior to ensure it doesn't negatively impact their team. They might take a moment to breathe before responding, or perhaps communicate their need for a brief pause, if necessary, rather than projecting their stress onto others.

An example of empathetic leadership in action might involve a team member who is consistently underperforming. Instead of immediately resorting to disciplinary measures, an empathetic leader would first seek to understand the root cause. They would schedule a private one-on-

one meeting and approach the conversation with curiosity and concern, rather than accusation. The leader might start by saying, "I've noticed that you seem to be struggling with some of your tasks lately, and I wanted to check in and see how you're doing. Is there anything going on that's making things difficult?" They would then listen attentively to the team members' responses. The issue might be a lack of clarity on expectations, a personal struggle outside of work, or a need for additional training or resources. By approaching the situation with empathy and a genuine desire to support, the leader can often uncover the real problem and work collaboratively towards a solution. This might involve providing additional coaching, adjusting work-loads temporarily, or connecting the employee with relevant support services. Such an approach not only helps the individual but also demonstrates to the entire team that the leader cares about their well-being and is committed to helping them succeed.

Creating a more supportive and inclusive team dynamic is a natural consequence of consistent empathetic behavior. When team members feel their leader understands and cares about their experiences, they are more likely to feel a sense of belonging. This is particularly crucial for fostering inclusion, as individuals from diverse backgrounds may have unique experiences and perspectives that require specific understanding and acknowledgment. An empathetic leader actively seeks to understand these differences and ensures that all voices are heard and respected. This involves being mindful of cultural nuances, communication styles, and personal circumstances that might influence an individual's approach to work.

For example, an empathetic leader might notice that a particular team member, who is new to the country, is hesitant to speak up in large group meetings. Rather than assuming disinterest or lack of ideas, the leader could make a conscious effort to create more inclusive communication channels. This might involve sending out meeting agendas in advance with an invitation to submit questions or comments beforehand or following up with the individual privately after the meeting to solicit their feedback. The leader might also explicitly state the value of diverse perspectives in team discussions, saying something like, "We have such a rich mix of backgrounds and experiences on this team, and I really want to make sure we're all benefiting from each other's unique insights. Please don't hesitate to share your thoughts, no matter how small you might think they are." This proactive approach to inclusion, driven by empathy, can transform a team into a truly collaborative and supportive environment where everyone feels empowered to contribute their best.

The consistent demonstration of empathy builds a reservoir of goodwill and trust. When team members know their leader will listen, understand, and act with consideration, they are more likely to be open, take risks, and commit to the team's goals. This isn't about being a pushover; it's about being a leader who is attuned to the human element of work, recognizing that people are motivated and engaged not just by rational directives, but by a sense of connection, respect, and genuine care. Empathy, therefore, is not a mere add-on to leadership; it is an essential, strategic driver of a psychologically safe, high-performing team. It is the quiet strength that enables a leader to navigate the complexities of human interaction, foster deep loyalty, and ultimately, build a team that is not only productive but also deeply engaged and resilient. In essence, empathetic leadership transforms the workplace from a mere collection of individuals into a cohesive unit, bound by mutual understanding and a shared commitment to collective success. This, in turn, creates a virtuous cycle where trust breeds openness, openness breeds innovation, and innovation drives sustained performance.

True leadership, at its core, is a delicate and dynamic balance between acknowledging our inherent human fallibility and accepting the full weight of our responsibilities. This balance is powerfully embodied in the intertwined principles of humility and accountability. These are not merely desirable character traits; they are foundational pillars that support and sustain a psychologically safe environment. Without them, even the most well-intentioned leader can inadvertently create a climate of fear, stagnation, or resentment.

Humility, in a leadership context, is far from a sign of weakness. It is, in fact, a profound strength derived from a clear-eyed understanding of one's own limitations and an equally clear appreciation for the capabilities and contributions of others. A humble leader recognizes that they do not possess a monopoly on good ideas, innovative solutions, or even accurate judgment. They understand that wisdom is distributed throughout an organization, residing in individuals who may hold different roles, possess diverse experiences, or approach problems from entirely unique vantage points. This self-awareness is critical for fostering psychological safety because it makes the leader approachable and receptive to feedback. When a leader openly admits they don't have all the answers, or that they might be mistaken, they create an invitation for others to speak up. This invitation is the very essence of psychological safety – the belief that one can speak up with ideas, questions, concerns, or even mistakes, without fear of punishment or humiliation. Consider a leader who, upon realizing a strategic decision they championed is not yielding the expected results, doesn't double down or deflect blame, but instead says, "It seems my initial assessment of this situation was incomplete. I'd like to hear everyone's perspectives on where we can course-correct." This admission of fallibility, delivered with genuine openness, signals that it is safe for others to voice their own potential missteps or to challenge existing assumptions. It cultivates an environment where learning is prioritized over perfection, and where diverse viewpoints are actively sought out, not just tolerated.

This openness is contagious. When leaders model humility, they encourage their teams to do the same. Team members who feel safe to admit they don't understand a concept or that they need help are more likely to be proactive in seeking clarification and support. They are also more likely to collaborate effectively, as they are less concerned with protecting their own perceived expertise and more focused on achieving a shared goal. A leader who is humble is more likely to listen actively, to ask clarifying questions, and to genuinely consider alternative approaches, rather than simply waiting for their turn to speak or defend their position. This active engagement with the ideas of others not only leads to better decision-making but also validates the contributions of each team member, reinforcing their sense of value and belonging. This is particularly important in rapidly evolving industries or complex problem-solving scenarios where no single individual can possibly possess all the necessary knowledge. The leader who embraces humility acknowledges this reality and actively leverages the collective intelligence of their team.

However, humility alone is insufficient for true leadership. It must be paired with a robust sense of accountability. Accountability, when exercised with care, is the commitment to taking ownership of one's actions, decisions, and their outcomes, and crucially, to learning from them. It's not about assigning blame or seeking scapegoats but about fostering a culture where responsibility is understood and embraced. A leader who is accountable demonstrates to their team that mistakes are not endpoints but opportunities for growth. This is where the crucial "balancing act" comes into play. A leader who is accountable, but not humble, might take ownership of a mistake in a rigid, unforgiving manner, perhaps leading to a climate of fear around errors. Conversely, a leader who is humble but lacks accountability might acknowledge shortcomings vaguely without taking concrete steps to rectify them or learn from them, leading to a sense of drift and unreliability.

The magic happens when humility and accountability are integrated. A leader who possesses both acknowledges their role in a setback ("I am accountable for the planning phase of this project, and it seems I underestimated the resources required") while also demonstrating humility in seeking solutions ("I need your help in re-evaluating our timeline and identifying potential workarounds"). This integrated approach creates a powerful signal to the team: "We are all in this together. We will own our contributions, learn from our missteps, and work collaboratively to find the best path forward." This fosters a profound sense of trust and shared purpose. When a leader admits they were wrong, takes responsibility, and then seeks input on how to fix it, they are demonstrating immense courage and integrity. This encourages team members to do the same, knowing that their own mistakes will be met with understanding and a focus on remediation, rather than punishment.

Consider a project that misses a critical deadline due to a series of communication breakdowns. A leader strong in both humility and accountability would not simply state, "We missed the deadline." Instead, they would likely initiate a post-mortem analysis with the team, starting with their own role. They might say, "I need to own my part in this. I recognize that I didn't establish clear communication protocols early enough, and I also didn't check in frequently enough to identify potential roadblocks. My apologies for that. Now, let's collectively dissect what happened from all angles. What could we have done differently? What were the barriers we faced, and how can we ensure this doesn't happen again?" This kind of statement is disarming. It invites honest reflection from the team because the leader has already opened the door by admitting their own fallibility and taking responsibility. The focus then shifts from "who is to blame?" to "what can we learn and how can we improve?" This process, driven by humble accountability, builds resilience. The team learns that even when things go wrong, they have a leader who will stand with them, take responsibility, and guide them toward improvement.

This culture of continuous improvement is a direct byproduct of this integrated approach. When leaders are humble, they are open to feedback about their own performance and decisions. When they are accountable, they act on that feedback and take responsibility for the outcomes. This creates a virtuous cycle. The team sees that providing constructive criticism or pointing out potential issues is valued and leads to positive change. They are more likely to offer suggestions, flag risks early, and proactively identify areas for improvement. This is invaluable in today's complex and fast-paced business environment. An organization that can continuously adapt and learn is an organization that thrives. A leader who embodies humility and accountability fosters this adaptive capacity by creating an environment where learning from experience, both successes and failures, is a shared commitment.

The impact of this on team morale and engagement is profound. When individuals feel that their leader is not only competent but also human, fallible, and committed to learning, they develop a deeper respect and loyalty. They are more likely to go the extra mile, to be innovative, and to feel a sense of ownership over their work and the team's collective success. This is because they feel seen, heard, and valued. They understand that their contributions are important and that even when mistakes occur, they will be met with a supportive and growth-oriented response. This, in turn, reduces the fear of failure, which is a significant inhibitor of creativity and risk-taking. Team members who are not afraid of making mistakes are more likely to experiment, to try new approaches, and to push the boundaries of what is possible.

Furthermore, the combination of humility and accountability fosters a more equitable and inclusive workplace. Humility helps leaders recognize and value the diverse perspectives and experiences of their team members. Accountability ensures that leadership decisions are not made in a vacuum and that leaders are answerable for the impact of those decisions on all members of the team, particularly those from underrepresented groups. When a leader is humble, they are more likely to actively solicit input from those who might typically be less vocal, ensuring that all voices are considered. When they are accountable, they are more likely to acknowledge and address any disparities or negative impacts that their decisions might have on different individuals or groups within the team. This creates a more just and supportive environment where everyone feels they have a fair opportunity to contribute and succeed.

Let's consider the practical application of this in performance management. A humble and accountable leader, when addressing performance issues, would not start with a punitive stance. They would first engage in a conversation, demonstrating humility by asking questions like, "What are your thoughts on how things are going with your current projects?" or "Are there any obstacles I might be unaware of that are impacting your work?" If performance does not indeed meet expectations, the leader would then step into accountability by clearly stating the observed impact and expectations. For example, "I've observed that the quality of the reports has been inconsistent lately, and this has led to delays in subsequent stages of the project. I'm accountable for ensuring that our team's work meets high standards, and I want to understand what's happening and how I can support you in meeting these expectations." The subsequent steps would then focus on collaborative problem-solving, setting clear goals, and providing necessary resources or coaching, all while holding the individual accountable for their part in the improvement process. This approach is constructive, respectful, and far more likely to lead to sustained positive change than a blame-centric model.

In essence, the leader who masterfully blends humility with accountability creates a powerful leadership signature. They are seen as credible because they admit their limitations and take ownership. They are trusted because they demonstrate integrity and a commitment to learning. They foster psychological safety because they create an environment where vulnerability is met with understanding and mistakes are viewed as stepping stones to growth. This is not a passive approach to leadership; it is an active, intentional cultivation of a culture that values honesty, responsibility, and continuous improvement. It's the bedrock upon which high-performing, resilient, and truly supportive teams are built. The absence of either humility or accountability leaves a leadership void, leading to either arrogance and disconnection or irresponsibility and disillusionment. It is their synergistic presence that transforms a leader from a manager of tasks into a cultivator of human potential and a champion of collective progress.

Chapter 5
Building Authentic Relationships through Meaningful Check-Ins

The simple act of checking in with your team members can be a profound tool for *empathetic leadership*, yet it is often relegated to a perfunctory update on tasks and deadlines. This subsection is dedicated to elevating that routine interaction, transforming it from a mere status report into a genuine opportunity for connection, understanding, and proactive support. Empathetic leaders recognize that their team members are individuals with lives that extend beyond the confines of their job descriptions, and that acknowledging and engaging with this broader reality is crucial for fostering trust, psychological safety, and ultimately, peak performance. Moving beyond the transactional nature of "what did you do?" to a more relational "how are you doing?" opens a vital channel for understanding the human element of work.

To initiate these human-centered check-ins effectively, the first step is a conscious shift in mindset. Instead of approaching the conversation with an agenda focused solely on project progress, leaders must cultivate genuine curiosity about the person on the other side of the screen or desk. This means preparing to listen more than you speak, and to ask questions that invite more than a one-word answer. The goal is to create a safe space where team members feel comfortable sharing not just their work-related accomplishments and roadblocks, but also their broader experiences, concerns, and even their aspirations. This isn't about prying into personal lives, but about acknowledging that a person's state of mind, their stress levels, or their personal challenges can significantly impact their professional output and well-being. A leader who demonstrates this awareness signals that they see their team members as whole individuals, not just as cogs in a machine.

One of the most effective ways to foster this deeper connection is by arming yourself with a toolkit of open-ended, empathy-driven conversation starters. These are not scripts to be followed rigidly, but rather springboards to encourage authentic dialogue. Instead of asking, "Are you on track with project X?", try something like, "How are you feeling about your workload this week, and is there anything that's feeling particularly challenging or energizing?" This subtle rephrasing shifts the focus from mere task completion to the individual's experience and emotional state. Other effective starters include: "What's been the most surprising or interesting thing you've encountered in your work recently?", "Is there anything you're grappling with that I might be able to help unblock?", or "On a scale of 1 to 10, how are you feeling about your overall experience with your current projects, and what's contributing to that rating?" The key is to ask questions that invite reflection and encourage elaboration, signaling that you are genuinely interested in the nuances of their experience.

Active listening is the indispensable companion to these probing questions. It's not enough to simply ask. You must be fully present, making eye contact (if in person or via video), nodding to show understanding, and resisting the urge to interrupt or jump in with solutions before the person has finished speaking. Paraphrasing what you've heard – for example, "So, if I'm understanding correctly, you're feeling overwhelmed by the competing deadlines and the lack of clarity on priority, is that right?" – not only confirms your understanding but also validates the speaker's experience. It shows that you've not only heard their words but have also processed their meaning. Beyond paraphrasing, emotional attunement is crucial.

If someone indicates frustration, acknowledge it by saying: "It seems that situation was frustrating for you." Recognizing and addressing an individual's emotional state serves as a fundamental component in establishing trust.

Consider the difference between a leader who asks, "How's the report coming along?" and receives a terse "Fine," and a leader who asks, "What's your experience been like working on the Q3 report? Are there any aspects that have been particularly smooth or perhaps presented some unexpected hurdles?" The latter approach is more likely to elicit a response that reveals, for instance, that the team member is struggling with data access, feeling isolated because they haven't collaborated with colleagues on this task, or feeling a lack of confidence in their analytical approach due to a gap in training. Without empathetic inquiry, these critical pieces of information, which directly affect the quality and timeliness of the report, remain hidden, leaving the leader unaware of underlying issues that could be addressed. By creating an opening for these details to emerge, the leader can then pivot to supportive action, helping with data access, facilitating a brief collaborative session, or suggesting a relevant training module.

The true power of these human-centered check-ins lies in their ability to proactively identify and address potential issues before they escalate into significant problems. When team members feel seen and heard, they are more likely to voice concerns early on. For example, if a team member is feeling burnt out, a regular, empathetic check-in might reveal this through their responses about energy levels or their ability to focus. A leader who is attuned to these signals can then intervene by adjusting workload, encouraging time off, or exploring the root causes of the burnout, such as unrealistic expectations or a lack of supportive resources. Without these regular, person-focused interactions, burnout could fester, leading to decreased productivity, increased errors, and ultimately, potential attrition, all of which could have been mitigated with timely, empathetic leadership.

Establishing a consistent rhythm for these check-ins is also vital. They should not be seen as a one-off event, but as an embedded practice within the leader's routine. Whether it's a brief, dedicated five-minute slot at the start of a one-on-one meeting, a quick virtual coffee break, or a designated moment at the end of a team huddle, the regularity communicates commitment. This consistent approach builds a predictable pattern of support and communication, making team members feel more secure and understood over time. The frequency might vary depending on team size and individual needs, but the underlying principle of regular, person-focused engagement remains constant. For larger teams, this might involve a mix of group check-ins that focus on general team sentiment and individual check-ins for more personal discussions.

Moreover, these check-ins serve as a critical feedback loop, not just for the leader to understand their team, but also for the team to understand the leader's priorities and perspective. When a leader shares a brief, genuine reflection on their own challenges or what they are learning, it further humanizes them. It reinforces the idea that vulnerability is a shared experience. For instance, a leader might say, "I'm still getting used to managing projects remotely, and I'm realizing I need to be more deliberate about creating informal connection points." This not only offers insight into the leader's own development journey but also implicitly validates the team's potential experiences with remote work challenges.

The structured yet flexible approach to these check-ins can be illustrated through a simple framework. Begin with a broad opening like, "Let's take a moment just to connect. How has your week been shaping up, beyond just the project tasks?" Listen attentively to the initial response. If it's a brief, surface-level answer, employ a follow-up question that probes gently: "Is there anything particularly exciting or challenging about what's on your plate right now?" or "What's something you're proud of accomplishing this week, big or small?" The goal is to create space for them to elaborate. If they share a challenge, your response should focus on understanding and support, rather than immediate problem-solving. "Thank you for sharing that. It sounds like you're feeling the pressure with

X, and that's understandable. What kind of support might be most helpful for you in navigating that?" This empowers the individual to be part of the solution. If they share a positive, focus on acknowledging and reinforcing it: "That's fantastic to hear about your success with Y! What do you think contributed most to that outcome?" This not only validates their achievement but also helps them identify their own strengths and successful strategies.

It's important to acknowledge that not every check-in will yield deep insights, and that's perfectly normal. Some days, team members might genuinely be focused on tasks and have little else to share, or they might be in a private moment where they prefer to keep their thoughts to themselves. The empathetic leader respects this. The offering of the space and the consistent invitation to connect are what matter. The absence of a deep revelation on any given day doesn't negate the value of the practice. It simply means that the door remains open for future conversations. The aim is to build a foundation of trust over time, so that when a significant issue does arise, the team member feels comfortable turning to their leader.

Furthermore, these human-centered check-ins can be a powerful tool for identifying potential interpersonal dynamics within a team that might be creating friction or hindering collaboration. If a leader consistently hears from one team member about difficulties in collaborating with another, or if there's a pattern of frustration directed towards a particular process or individual, these check-ins provide an early warning system. A leader who is aware of these undercurrents can then discreetly investigate, perhaps by speaking with other team members (while maintaining confidentiality) or by facilitating a team discussion on communication protocols and best collaborative practices. Proactive intervention based on these subtle cues, identified through empathetic listening, can prevent minor team friction from escalating into more significant conflicts that damage morale and productivity.

The impact of consistent, empathetic check-ins extends beyond individual well-being to the broader team culture. When these interactions become a norm, they foster an environment of openness and mutual respect. Team members begin to see their leader not just as a manager of tasks, but as a supportive ally. This, in turn, can encourage team members to extend similar consideration to one another, creating a more cohesive and psychologically safe collective. It shifts the team dynamic from one where individual performance is paramount to one where collective well-being and support are equally valued. This creates a stronger, more resilient team that is better equipped to navigate challenges together.

In essence, initiating human-centered check-ins is about intentionally cultivating connection in the workplace. It requires a conscious effort to move beyond the transactional and embrace the relational. By arming yourself with empathetic questions, practicing active and deep listening, and committing to a consistent rhythm of these interactions, you build trust, uncover potential issues early, and foster a team environment where individuals feel valued, understood, and supported. This is not a soft skill; it is a fundamental leadership practice that underpins engagement, resilience, and sustained high performance. It is the daily, tangible manifestation of leading with the human at the center.

Empathetic questioning is far more than a simple inquiry; it's a deliberate and skilled approach to drawing out insights, understanding nuances, and fostering a sense of psychological safety. It's about asking questions that don't just seek information, but that also convey respect, curiosity, and a genuine desire to understand the other person's world. This is the cornerstone of building deep, trusting relationships in the workplace, moving beyond superficial interactions to cultivate a truly supportive environment. When leaders employ empathetic questioning, they signal that they see their team members not just as contributors to tasks, but as complex individuals with unique perspectives, feelings, and needs. This fundamental shift in interaction can transform team dynamics, unlocking greater collaboration, engagement, and a more resilient workforce.

The core of empathetic questioning lies in its openness. Unlike closed questions that can be answered with simple "yes" or "no," open-ended questions invite elaboration, encouraging the respondent to share more. For instance, instead of asking, "Did you finish the presentation?", an empathetic leader might ask, "How are you feeling about the progress on the presentation? What has been your experience working on it?" This subtle alteration shifts the focus from a binary outcome to the individual's journey and their subjective experience. It opens the door for them to discuss challenges they encountered, insights they gained, or even how the task made them feel – whether it was invigorating, tedious, or overwhelming. The invitation to share personal reflections, rather than just task completion status, is what makes the question empathetic. It demonstrates that the leader values the process and the person involved, not just the final product.

To further illustrate, consider a situation where a team member seems disengaged or is producing work that is below their usual standard. A non-empathetic approach might involve direct criticism or demands for explanation. An empathetic leader, however, would use questioning to understand the underlying cause. They might start with something like, "I've noticed a shift in your usual engagement lately, and I wanted to check in. How have things been for you this past week?" This is an invitation to share, not an accusation. If the response is still guarded, a follow-up question could be, "Is there anything that's been particularly draining your energy or occupying your thoughts outside of our immediate work that you feel comfortable sharing?" This acknowledges that personal circumstances can impact professional performance without prying. The key is to create a safe space where sharing is an option, not an obligation, and where the leader's intention is clearly supportive.

Validating feelings is another crucial element of empathetic questioning. Often, when people express a difficulty, they are looking for acknowledgment of their emotional experience as much as they are for a solution. Questions designed to validate can include phrases like, "It sounds like that situation was really frustrating for you. Is that right?" or "I can imagine that must have felt quite overwhelming. How are you processing that?" By reflecting on the perceived emotion and seeking confirmation, the leader shows they are not just hearing the words but also trying to understand the emotional impact. This validation can be incredibly powerful, helping the individual feel understood and less alone in their struggle. It's a way of saying, "I see your struggle, and it's okay to feel this way." This builds a profound level of trust, as the team member learns that their emotional responses are recognized and accepted.

Encouraging reflection through questioning helps individuals gain deeper self-awareness and identify their own potential solutions. Instead of immediately jumping in with advice, an empathetic leader might ask, "Given what you've experienced with this task, what are your thoughts on how you might approach it differently next time?" or "What insights have you gained from this challenge that could be useful for future projects?" These questions empower the team member to tap into their own problem-solving capabilities. They foster a sense of agency and ownership over their development, which is far more sustainable than relying on external guidance. It shifts the dynamic from a dependency model to one of partnership and growth, where the leader acts as a facilitator of the team member's own learning process.

Collaborative problem-solving is the natural evolution of empathetic questioning and validation. Once a challenge or concern has been clearly articulated and understood, the leader can pivot to a collaborative approach. This might involve questions like, "What kind of support do you think would be most helpful for you in navigating this?" or "Let's brainstorm some options together. What are your initial ideas on how we can address this?" This approach ensures that the solutions developed are relevant to the individual's needs and context, and it reinforces the idea that the leader and the team member are working together as a team. It's about co-creating solutions, rather than imposing them. This shared ownership increases the likelihood of successful implementation and reinforces the supportive relationship between leader and team member.

Consider the impact of these questioning techniques on a team member facing a particularly complex technical problem. A leader who asks, "Are you stuck on the coding aspect of this?" might get a simple "yes." However, a leader employing empathetic questioning might ask, "Tell me about your experience debugging that section. What have you tried so far, and what feels most challenging about it right now?" This invites the team member to articulate their process, their thought patterns, and the specific hurdles they're encountering. It might reveal that the difficulty isn't just in the coding itself, but perhaps in a lack of clear documentation, an unfamiliarity with a particular library, or a misunderstanding of the overall architecture. By understanding these nuances, the leader can offer more targeted support – perhaps suggesting a relevant online resource, pairing them with a colleague who has expertise in that area, or facilitating a brief session to review the code together. This approach demonstrates a commitment to helping the team member overcome the obstacle, rather than simply ticking a box for problem resolution.

Furthermore, empathetic questioning can be a powerful tool for identifying potential areas of growth and development for team members. By asking questions that encourage self-assessment and forward-thinking, leaders can help individuals pinpoint skills they want to develop or areas where they feel they need more experience. For example, during a performance review or a one-on-one, a leader might ask, "Looking ahead, what are you most excited to learn or get better at in your role?" or "If you could have a 'stretch' assignment that would help you grow, what might that look like?" These questions not only provide valuable insights into an individual's career aspirations but also signal that the leader is invested in their long-term professional development. This can significantly boost morale and loyalty, as team members feel their potential is recognized and nurtured.

The art of asking questions also involves understanding the context and the individual. The same question can elicit very different responses depending on the relationship, the environment, and the individual's personality. An empathetic leader is attuned to these factors. They understand that some team members might be more introverted and prefer to process their thoughts before speaking, while others are more extroverted and comfortable sharing spontaneously. Therefore, the leader might offer a heads-up before a meeting: "I'd like to discuss your work on project X and get your thoughts on how we can optimize it. Please feel free to jot down any initial ideas beforehand if that helps." This provides structure for those who need it, without imposing a rigid format.

Moreover, empathetic questions should be delivered with genuine curiosity and without judgment. The tone of voice, body language, and facial expressions all play a crucial role. A question like, "Why did you do it that way?" can sound accusatory, whereas "Can you walk me through your thought process for that approach?" is much more collaborative and inviting. The leader must convey an attitude of "I'm here to understand," rather than "I'm here to find fault." This non-judgmental stance is essential for creating psychological safety that encourages honest and open communication. When team members know they won't be judged for their responses, they are far more likely to share their true thoughts and feelings.

It's also important to recognize that sometimes, the most empathetic response to a question is not to ask another question, but to offer silence. After asking an open-ended question, giving the team member time to formulate their thoughts without interruption is a powerful form of active listening. This pause can feel uncomfortable for the leader, who might be tempted to fill the silence, but it is often during these moments of quiet reflection that the most meaningful responses emerge. The leader's ability to remain present and patient, demonstrating that they are willing to wait for the best possible answer, reinforces the message that they truly value what the team member has to say.

Chapter 6
Using Vulnerability to Foster Trust and Resilience in Teams

A practical application of empathetic questioning can be seen in how leaders handle mistakes or setbacks. Instead of focusing solely on the error, the empathetic leader uses questions to understand the context and extract learning. For instance, after a project misses a deadline, a leader might ask, "Let's debrief this. What were the key challenges we encountered in meeting the deadline for project Y?" Then, following up with, "What lessons can we take away from this experience that will help us plan more effectively for future projects?" and crucially, "What support do you feel you need to prevent similar issues from arising again?" These questions shift the focus from blame to collective learning and improvement. They demonstrate that the leader sees setbacks as opportunities for growth, not as failures to be punished. This fosters a culture where mistakes are viewed as learning opportunities, encouraging innovation and reducing the fear of failure that can stifle creativity.

Ultimately, mastering empathetic questioning is about cultivating a mindset of genuine curiosity and care. It requires commitment to seeing team members as whole individuals, with complex lives that influence their work. By honing the ability to ask open-ended, validating, and reflective questions, leaders can unlock deeper understanding, foster trust, and provide more tailored and effective support. This practice not only enhances individual well-being and performance but also contributes to a more cohesive, resilient, and high-performing team culture. It's an ongoing skill, honed through practice and a sincere desire to connect on a human level, transforming the daily interactions that shape the workplace experience.

The journey toward empathetic leadership is intrinsically linked to the willingness of leaders to be vulnerable. In many traditional organizational cultures, leadership has been equated with unwavering strength, omniscience, and a distinct lack of personal fallibility. This often creates a paradoxical environment where leaders are expected to foster open communication and psychological safety, yet are rarely seen demonstrating the very qualities that enable such an environment to flourish. However, a truly empathetic leader understands that vulnerability is not a weakness, but rather a powerful catalyst for connection, trust, and authentic engagement. By intentionally modeling vulnerability, leaders can dismantle the unspoken barriers that prevent team members from sharing their own challenges, uncertainties, and even mistakes, thereby cultivating a workplace where openness is not just permitted but actively encouraged.

The act of a leader admitting they don't have all the answers, or that they are struggling with a particular aspect of their role, can be profoundly disarming and humanizing. This isn't about oversharing personal dramas or creating a burden for the team, but rather about strategically and appropriately revealing aspects of one's own learning process and moments of doubt. For instance, during a team meeting where a complex problem is being discussed, a leader might say, "I've been thinking a lot about how to approach this, and I'm still wrestling with the best path forward. I've tried a couple of things that haven't quite hit the mark. I'd really value your perspectives on how you're seeing this challenge." This statement does several things: it acknowledges that the problem is difficult, it signals that the leader is also engaged in problem-solving and not detached from the struggle, and most importantly, it explicitly invites input and collaboration. By showing that they, too, are navigating uncertainty, leaders give permission to others to do the same. This subtle yet significant act can shift the team's dynamic from one where individuals feel the need to always present a facade of competence to one where collective problem-solving and mutual support are the norm.

Admitting mistakes is another cornerstone of normalizing vulnerability. Every professional, regardless of their seniority, will inevitably make errors. The crucial difference lies in how these mistakes are handled. When a leader openly acknowledges a misstep – perhaps a decision that didn't yield the expected results, or a misjudgment in planning – it sends a powerful message. Imagine a scenario where a project deadline was missed due to an initial estimation error made by the leader. Instead of deflecting blame or remaining silent, the leader might address the team with something like, "I want to take responsibility for my part in us missing the deadline on the X project. My initial assessment of the timeline was overly optimistic, and I should have accounted for more variables. I've learned from this, and going forward, I'll be more rigorous in our planning phase." This admission serves multiple purposes. It demonstrates accountability, a highly valued leadership trait. It also reduces the fear of repercussion for others who might make a mistake. If the leader can own up to their errors, then team members are more likely to feel safe admitting their own, allowing for a more honest and productive debriefing and learning process. This creates a culture where mistakes are seen not as terminal failures, but as opportunities for collective growth and process improvement.

Seeking help is a direct demonstration of vulnerability and a powerful way to build trust. When leaders are perceived as always having the answers and never needing assistance, it can create a sense of isolation and discourage team members from asking for support themselves. Conversely, a leader who proactively seeks input or guidance from their team normalizes the act of needing help. For example, when preparing for a significant presentation to external stakeholders, a leader might approach a team member and say, "I'm really focused on delivering a compelling narrative for this client, but I'm finding it challenging to distill some of the technical details into a clear, engaging message for a non-technical audience. I've always admired your ability to explain complex ideas simply. Would you be willing to look over my draft and give me some feedback on how to make it more accessible?" This request not only acknowledges the leader's own limitations but also explicitly values the skills of the team member. It fosters a sense of partnership and mutual reliance, reinforcing the idea that everyone's contributions are valuable, regardless of their role or title. It also signals that seeking help is a strength, indicating a commitment to achieving the best possible outcome.

Expressing constructive emotions is perhaps one of the most challenging, yet most impactful, aspects of modeling vulnerability. While workplaces are professional environments, they are also populated by human beings who experience a range of emotions. Suppressing emotions entirely can lead to a sterile and inauthentic atmosphere. Empathetic leaders, however, learn to express their feelings in a way that is appropriate to the context and that fosters understanding, rather than drama. This doesn't mean lamenting over personal setbacks but rather acknowledging how a situation might impact one's state of mind or drive. For instance, after a particularly challenging quarter or a difficult client interaction, a leader might share with their team, "I have to admit, this past week has been quite draining, and I've felt a sense of frustration trying to navigate these unexpected hurdles. However, seeing how we've all pulled together to keep things moving forward has been incredibly inspiring. It reminds me why I value working with such a dedicated group." This type of sharing validates the collective experience of challenge, acknowledges the leader's own emotional response without dwelling on it, and immediately pivots to recognizing the team's resilience and effort. It creates a shared emotional landscape, where struggles are acknowledged and overcome together, rather than being individually borne in silence. This approach helps to demystify leadership and makes the leader more relatable.

Building a safe space for openness requires more than just occasional admission of weakness. It necessitates a consistent and intentional effort to create an environment where authenticity is the expected norm. This means actively listening when team members express concerns, even if those concerns are about the leader themselves or the organization's direction. It also means responding with empathy and a willingness to explore the issue, rather than defensiveness. When a team member feels safe enough to say, "I'm concerned about the pace of this project, and I'm worried it's leading to burnout within the team," an empathetic leader will not dismiss this as a mere complaint. Instead, they might respond, "Thank you for bringing that to my attention. I appreciate you sharing that concern. Can you tell me more about what you're observing and how you feel it's impacting the team?" This response validates the team member's feelings, shows respect for their observation, and opens the door for a constructive dialogue to address the underlying issue. It signals that the leader is open to feedback and committed to the well-being of the team, which in turn encourages greater transparency.

The concept of "appropriate" vulnerability is key here. Leaders are not expected to share every personal struggle. The vulnerability that fosters a safe space is that which is relevant to the work context and serves to build connection or illustrate a point about leadership, resilience, or problem-solving. For example, during a discussion about overcoming project setbacks, a leader might share a brief anecdote from their experience where they faced a similar challenge and how they navigated it, including the moments of doubt they experienced. This is different from recounting a personal crisis unrelated to work. The focus remains on the professional impact and the lessons learned. The objective is to make the leader more human and accessible, not to create an audience for personal confessions. The boundary between personal and professional is maintained, but the wall between leader and team member is lowered.

Furthermore, leaders can create opportunities for vulnerability by fostering a culture of continuous learning. This involves encouraging experimentation, recognizing that experimentation often involves trial and error. When a new initiative is launched or a new process is introduced, a leader can set the tone by admitting their own learning curve. "As we roll out this new CRM system, I'm still getting up to speed on all of its features," a leader might say. "I'm sure there will be moments where we all need to learn from each other as we figure out the best ways to utilize it. Please don't hesitate to share any tips or shortcuts you discover, or if you're struggling with something, let's tackle it together." This proactive acknowledgment of the learning process reduces the pressure on individuals to appear as experts from day one. It creates a collective sense of endeavor, where the team is united in its pursuit of mastery, and where seeking clarification or admitting a lack of understanding is a natural part of that journey.

The impact of a leader's vulnerability extends to how they handle conflict or disagreement within the team. Instead of suppressing dissenting voices or imposing their own will, an empathetic leader will acknowledge the validity of different perspectives, even if they don't agree with them. This can involve admitting that they don't have all the answers to a complex strategic decision, or that they understand why a particular team member might be resistant to a proposed change. For instance, during a debate about a new marketing strategy, a leader might say, "I hear your reservations about this approach, Sarah. I understand that you feel it might alienate a segment of our loyal customer base, and I recognize the validity of your concern. While I believe this new direction has significant potential, I also value your experience and insight. Let's talk further about how we can mitigate those risks you've identified." This demonstrates that the leader is open to being persuaded, that they value diverse viewpoints, and that they are willing to engage in dialogue to find the best collective solution. It transforms conflict from a threat into a source of valuable insight.

Moreover, creating a safe space for vulnerability means that leaders must be prepared to handle the vulnerability shared by others with care and respect. If a team member shares a personal struggle that is impacting their work, the leader's response is critical. This involves listening without judgment, maintaining confidentiality, and offering appropriate support, which might include flexibility in work arrangements, connecting them with HR resources, or simply offering a listening ear. For example, if an employee confides that they are experiencing significant stress due to family health issues, the leader's response could be, "Thank you for trusting me with this. I'm sorry to hear you're going through such a difficult time. Your well-being is important, and I want to see how we can best support you through this. What kind of adjustments do you think would be most helpful for you at work right now?" This empathetic response acknowledges the gravity of the situation, prioritizes the employee's welfare, and opens a collaborative discussion about practical solutions. It reinforces that the leader's commitment to vulnerability extends to creating a supportive environment for their team members when they choose to share their own challenges.

The culture of authenticity is not built overnight; it is cultivated through consistent actions and intentional communication. Leaders who openly share their learning journeys, admit when they need help, and express their emotions appropriately are laying the groundwork for a more resilient and engaged workforce. They are demonstrating that it is safe to be human, to make mistakes, and to seek support. This, in turn, empowers team members to bring their whole selves to work, to contribute their unique perspectives, and to collaborate more effectively. The paradoxical truth is that by revealing their own imperfections, leaders project an image of greater strength, credibility, and trustworthiness, fostering a workplace where genuine connection and open dialogue can truly thrive. This uncovers the foundational elements for deeper empathy, allowing leaders not only to understand but also to be understood, creating a more harmonious and productive working environment for everyone.

Empathetic leadership extends beyond understanding individual emotions; it critically involves the proactive management of the team's collective workload to prevent the insidious creep of burnout. As a leader, your role is not merely to assign tasks, but to orchestrate them in a way that fosters sustained productivity and well-being. This requires a strategic approach to how work is distributed, assessed, and managed, ensuring that the demands placed upon your team are challenging yet achievable, and that the inevitable pressures of work do not escalate into chronic stress. The essence of this practice lies in recognizing that a team's capacity is not an inexhaustible resource, and that thoughtful management of tasks is paramount to preserving both individual health and organizational success.

The first crucial step in actively managing workloads is to gain a comprehensive understanding of the tasks at hand and the capacity of each team member. This is not a one-time assessment, but an ongoing process that requires diligent attention. Leaders must develop clear visibility into the projects, deadlines, and ongoing responsibilities assigned to everyone. Tools such as project management software, shared task boards, or even regular one-on-one check-ins can provide this much-needed oversight. However, simply knowing what needs to be done is insufficient. It is equally important to understand the complexity and estimated time commitment for each task, as well as the current bandwidth of your team members. This often involves having open conversations about how individuals are feeling about their current workload, not just in terms of quantity, but also in terms of the cognitive and emotional energy required. For instance, a leader might initiate a conversation by asking, "On a scale of one to ten, how manageable does your current workload feel this week? And can you elaborate on what makes it feel that way?" This simple question, coupled with active listening, can reveal a great deal about potential bottlenecks or areas where an individual might be silently struggling.

Chapter 7
The Balance of Work and Well-Being

Identifying potential overload is an art form that relies on keen observation and empathetic inquiry. Burnout often begins subtly, with signs like decreased engagement, increased irritability, missed deadlines, or a decline in the quality of work. These are not isolated incidents but often indicators of a team or individual operating beyond their sustainable capacity. As a leader, it's your responsibility to look for these patterns. Are team members consistently working late? Are they expressing a lack of motivation or enthusiasm for tasks they once enjoyed? Do they seem withdrawn or less communicative during team interactions? Beyond these behavioral cues, it's also vital to understand the nature of the work itself. Are there periods of intense, concentrated effort that are not adequately balanced with more manageable phases? Is the team consistently being asked to perform under unrealistic time pressures? Proactive identification requires a willingness to have difficult conversations. It might mean addressing a team member who is consistently the first to arrive and the last to leave, and gently inquiring about their workload and stress levels, offering support rather than assuming their dedication is simply an admirable trait. For example, you might say, "I've noticed you've been putting in very long hours lately, and I really appreciate your commitment. However, I'm also concerned about your well-being. Can we chat about your current projects and see if there are ways to redistribute or adjust the load to ensure you have a sustainable pace?"

Once potential overload is identified, the next critical step is implementing strategies for effective workload management. This involves a multifaceted approach that includes prioritization, delegation, and the judicious use of the word "no."

Prioritization is a cornerstone of workload management. Not all tasks are created equal, and a leader must guide the team in understanding which tasks are most critical and which can be deferred or re-evaluated. This requires a clear understanding of organizational goals and priorities. Techniques such as the Eisenhower Matrix (Urgent/Important) can be invaluable for both the leader and the team to categorize tasks and focus energy where it will have the greatest impact. However, the leader's role in prioritization is not just about defining the order; it's about communicating *why* that order is important. Explaining the strategic rationale behind prioritizing one project over another helps the team understand the bigger picture and feel more invested in the chosen direction. When faced with competing demands, a leader might convene a brief meeting to discuss upcoming tasks and collectively decide on the most effective sequencing, saying, "We have these three key initiatives for the next quarter. Based on our strategic objectives, the client deadline for Project A is our absolute priority. Project B is important for long-term growth, but it can afford a slightly more flexible timeline. Project C, while valuable, is currently secondary. Let's focus our primary energy on Project A, ensuring we deliver exceptionally, and then strategically allocate resources to Project B."

Delegation is another powerful tool, often underutilized by leaders who feel they can do a task better or faster themselves. Effective delegation is not simply offloading work; it's about empowering team members, developing their skills, and leveraging the collective strengths of the team. This requires careful consideration of who is best suited for a particular task, not just in terms of their current skills but also their potential for growth. When delegating, provide clear instructions, context, desired outcomes, and the necessary resources and authority. Crucially, establish check-in points to monitor progress without micromanaging. A leader might delegate a complex report to a developing team member by saying, "Sarah, I'd like you to take the lead on compiling the quarterly sales report. I've always been impressed with your analytical skills. I'll provide you with the raw data and the template from last year. The key is to identify the top three growth trends and provide supporting data points. Let's plan to have a quick sync on Tuesday to review your initial findings and address any questions you might have." This approach not only assigns the task but also offers support and a clear path for feedback, fostering confidence and skill development.

Perhaps one of the most challenging, yet essential, aspects of workload management is the ability to say "no." In environments that often encourage a "can-do" attitude, declining new requests or projects can feel counterintuitive. However, an empathetic leader understands that overcommitment leads to diminished quality, increased stress, and ultimately, burnout.

Saying "no" is not an act of refusal; it's an act of responsible resource management and a commitment to the well-being of the team. This requires the leader to be clear about the team's current capacity and to have the courage to communicate limitations constructively. When faced with a new request that exceeds capacity, a leader might respond by outlining current commitments and proposing alternatives or a revised timeline. For example, "I understand the importance of this new marketing campaign, and I appreciate you bringing it to us. Currently, the team is fully engaged in delivering the critical product launch next month, which requires our undivided attention to ensure its success. Given our current commitments, we wouldn't be able to give this new campaign the focus it deserves. Would it be possible to revisit this in two months, or perhaps we can discuss a scaled-back version that we can manage alongside our existing priorities?" This response acknowledges the request, explains the constraint, and offers a path forward, demonstrating both a commitment to the new opportunity and a responsibility to the existing workload.

Furthermore, creating a culture where workload management is a shared responsibility is vital. This involves encouraging team members to communicate their capacity and to support one another. Leaders can foster this by promoting open dialogue about workload during team meetings and one-on-ones. When a team member voices concern about being overloaded, the leader should treat this as valuable feedback, not a complaint. This feedback can inform decisions about resource allocation, project scope, or even the need to push back on unrealistic expectations from other departments or stakeholders. For instance, during a team retrospective, if a team member expresses feeling overwhelmed, the leader can facilitate a discussion: "Thanks for sharing that, John. It sounds like you're feeling stretched thin. For the rest of the team, how are you feeling about your current workload? Are there any bottlenecks or areas where we can help redistribute tasks or offer support?" This encourages a collective awareness of workload and promotes peer support, reinforcing the idea that team success is built on sustainable effort from everyone.

The impact of proactive workload management on preventing burnout is profound. When leaders consistently prioritize, delegate effectively, and manage capacity, they create an environment where individuals can perform at their best without compromising their health and well-being. This leads to higher job satisfaction, increased engagement, reduced turnover, and ultimately, a more resilient and productive team. It demonstrates to the team that their leader values them not just for their output, but for their overall health and long-term contribution. This mindful approach to task management is a direct manifestation of empathetic leadership, translating empathy into tangible actions that safeguard the human capital of the organization. It's about building a sustainable work environment where success is achieved through smart, strategic effort, not through the exhaustion of its people. The leader's commitment to this practice signals that the team's well-being is not an afterthought, but a fundamental component of how work is done. This, in turn, builds a strong foundation of trust and respect, where team members feel secure and valued, knowing their leader is actively working to create an environment that supports both their professional growth and their personal health. This proactive stance against burnout is not just a management strategy; it's a critical element of ethical and effective leadership in the modern workplace, ensuring that the pursuit of organizational goals does not come at the expense of the people who drive them. It is through these deliberate actions that an empathetic leader cultivates a thriving, healthy, and high-performing team capable of navigating challenges and achieving sustainable success.

In the intricate dance of leadership, where the well-being of the team is paramount, the concept of protecting personal time emerges as a non-negotiable pillar of empathetic practice. This isn't merely about efficiency or time management; it's a fundamental acknowledgment of our shared humanity and the intrinsic need for rest, rejuvenation, and a life beyond the confines of our professional roles. As leaders, we are not just architects of projects and strategies; we are custodians of our team's vitality. This responsibility extends to actively safeguarding their personal time, a critical element in preventing the insidious creep of burnout and fostering a sustainable, healthy work environment.

The foundational element of protecting personal time lies in the leader's own behavior – the powerful, often unspoken, communication that emanates from our daily actions. We must become living embodiments of healthy boundaries. This means consciously modeling the very behaviors we wish to see in our teams. Consider the subtle yet significant impact of responding to emails at 11 PM on a Saturday or sending urgent requests on a Sunday afternoon. While such actions might be perceived by some as dedication, they inadvertently set a dangerous precedent. They communicate, however unintentionally, that this level of constant availability is not only expected but perhaps even required for success. This can create a pervasive undercurrent of pressure, where team members feel compelled to mirror this behavior, sacrificing their own personal time and, consequently, their well-being. Empathetic leaders understand that their personal time is not an open invitation for work-related intrusions. Instead, they treat it as sacred, recognizing that periods of genuine disconnection are vital for cognitive recovery, creative thinking, and maintaining overall mental and physical health. This commitment to personal time protection is not a sign of disengagement; rather, it is a strategic investment in long-term effectiveness and personal sustainability.

To translate this into tangible action, leaders must proactively establish clear expectations regarding availability and response times outside of regular work hours. It starts with transparent dialogue and practices that support healthy work-life integration, rather than nonstop availability. Make disconnecting not just allowed but encouraged. This can be achieved through a variety of methods. For instance, at the commencement of a new project or even at the beginning of a team meeting, a leader can explicitly state their approach to communication outside of core working hours. Phrases like, "I generally monitor emails during business hours and will respond to urgent matters as soon as possible. For non-urgent queries received after 6 PM or on weekends, I aim to address them during the next working day," can set a clear and respectful tone. This clarity removes ambiguity and empowers team members to do the same, knowing that their own personal time will be respected.

Furthermore, the act of *not* sending emails late at night or over the weekend is a powerful signal. When a leader refrains from sending non-urgent communications during personal time, they are sending a clear message: "My time is my own, and yours is too." This is not about shirking responsibility; it is about demonstrating respect for the boundaries that are essential for well-being. If a task or project requires immediate attention outside of normal hours, a leader might consider using scheduling features for emails, queuing them up to be sent during the next business day. This maintains the urgency for the task itself without imposing it on the recipient's personal time. This thoughtful approach shows a deep understanding of the psychological impact of constant digital connectivity. It acknowledges that the mental load of receiving work-related communications during downtime can prevent true relaxation and recovery, leading to cumulative stress and reduced effectiveness over time.

Beyond digital communication, the encouragement of taking breaks and truly disconnecting is equally vital. This involves more than just verbal encouragement; it requires active support and creating an environment where breaks are seen as productive necessities, not signs of slacking. Leaders can champion this by openly taking their own breaks, stepping away from their desks for lunch, or even taking short walks during the day. When a team member is seen taking a break, a leader should offer a smile or a nod of encouragement, reinforcing that this is a valued part of the workday. This also extends vacation time. Empathetic leaders actively encourage their team members to utilize their accrued vacation days.

This might involve proactively reminding individuals about their remaining leave, discussing upcoming holidays, or even helping to plan coverage for their absence to alleviate any perceived burden of taking time off. The message here is clear: "Your well-being is a priority, and that includes taking time to recharge and step away from work." This proactive encouragement combats the guilt or anxiety that some employees feel when considering time off, particularly in environments where longer hours are subtly valued.

It is crucial to understand that promoting the protection of personal time is not about advocating for reduced work effort or a lack of commitment. Instead, it is about fostering a more sustainable and humane approach to work. It is about recognizing that individuals are multifaceted beings with lives, families, hobbies, and personal needs that extend far beyond their professional identities. When leaders champion the protection of personal time, they are signaling that work is an important part of life, but not its entirety. This cultivates a culture that deeply respects individual well-being, preventing the erosion of work-life integration and, by extension, the erosion of the individual's spirit and capacity. It's about building a work environment where individuals can thrive, not just survive, and where their personal time is a protected space for them to nurture their lives outside of work, ultimately making them more engaged, creative, and resilient when they *are* at work.

The impact of this boundary setting extends beyond the individual team member; it influences the entire team dynamic and the organization's overall culture. When leaders consistently model and reinforce healthy personal time boundaries, they create a ripple effect. Team members are more likely to feel empowered to set their own boundaries, leading to a more balanced workforce. This can reduce the instances of presenteeism, where employees are physically present but mentally disengaged due to exhaustion, and absenteeism, where employees are absent due to stress-related illnesses. A team that respects personal time is a team that is less prone to burnout, more likely to be engaged, and ultimately, more productive in the long run. It fosters an environment of psychological safety, where employees feel secure in their ability to disconnect without fear of negative repercussions.

To further solidify these practices, leaders can implement specific strategies such as establishing "no-meeting" blocks during the day or week to allow for focused work or encouraging "deep work" sessions where distractions are minimized. These practices, when combined with clear communication of expectations around out-of-hours availability, create a robust framework for protecting personal time. It's about building intentionality into the workday, ensuring that both professional responsibilities and personal well-being are given the consideration they deserve.

Consider the scenario where a team member is consistently working late and appearing fatigued. An empathetic leader, attuned to the importance of personal time, wouldn't simply compliment their "dedication." Instead, they would initiate a conversation to understand the root cause. "I've noticed you've been staying quite late recently, and I appreciate your commitment. However, I'm also mindful of ensuring you have a healthy work-life balance. Is there anything about your current workload or processes that's contributing to these extended hours? Perhaps we can look at ways to streamline or redistribute tasks." This approach shifts the focus from simply observing long hours to actively addressing the underlying factors that might be encroaching on personal time. It opens the door for collaborative problem-solving, where the leader and the team member can jointly identify solutions, whether it's reprioritizing tasks, seeking additional support, or improving time management strategies.

Another critical aspect is to ensure that the organization's policies and practices support the protection of personal time. This includes having clear guidelines on overtime, ensuring that vacation policies are generous and actively promoted, and that there are no implicit or explicit pressures to be constantly "on." Leaders play a crucial role in advocating for these policies and ensuring they are implemented effectively within their teams. They can be the champions for a culture that values rest and rejuvenation, understanding that sustained high performance is a marathon, not a sprint, and requires periods of genuine recovery.

The commitment to protecting personal time is an ongoing practice, not a one-time fix. It requires continuous vigilance, open communication, and a willingness to adapt as circumstances change. By prioritizing and modeling healthy boundaries, leaders not only safeguard their teams from burnout but also cultivate a more respectful, sustainable, and ultimately, more effective work environment. This dedication to individual well-being is a hallmark of empathetic leadership, demonstrating that success is best achieved when people are empowered to live full, balanced lives, both inside and outside the workplace. It is in this consistent, deliberate effort that the true strength of empathetic leadership is revealed, building trust and fostering a deep sense of value within the team. This isn't just good management; it's profoundly human leadership that recognizes the essential connection between personal well-being and professional contribution. When individuals feel their personal time is respected, they are more likely to bring their best selves to work, contributing to a more positive and productive organizational culture. This creates a virtuous cycle where empathy leads to respect, respect leads to well-being, and well-being fuels sustained high performance.

Chapter 8
Practical Tools and Policy Frameworks for Support

Navigating conversations about mental health and well-being within the workplace is one of the most critical, yet often challenging aspects of modern leadership. It requires a delicate balance of empathy, clarity, and professionalism. To equip leaders and HR professionals with the confidence and practical tools needed for these sensitive dialogues, we've developed a series of conversation scripts. These are not rigid dictates, but rather flexible frameworks, designed to be adapted to individual situations and personalities. The goal is to provide a starting point, a way to initiate these vital conversations with care and competence.

Initiating a Conversation with a Distressed Team Member

When you observe a team member exhibiting signs of distress – perhaps a noticeable change in demeanor, decreased productivity, increased absenteeism, or withdrawal from team activities – it's crucial to address it proactively, rather than waiting for a crisis. The first step is to create a private, comfortable, and confidential space for the conversation. This could be an empty meeting room, your office with the door closed, or even a virtual meeting on a secure platform. The opening of the conversation is paramount; it sets the tone and can either encourage openness or create defensiveness.

A good opening focuses on observed behaviors and expresses genuine concern, without making assumptions or diagnoses.

Script Example 1: Expressing Concern Based on Observation

"Hi [Employee Name], thanks for taking the time to chat. I wanted to check in with you. I've noticed over the past [period, e.g., few weeks] that you seem [describe observed behavior neutrally, e.g., a bit quieter than usual, or that your engagement in team meetings has changed]. I also noticed [mention a specific work-related observation, e.g., that a few deadlines have been missed recently, or that your usual level of input isn't as prominent]. I wanted to reach out and see how you're doing, both professionally and personally. My main concern is your well-being, and I want to ensure you have the support you need."

Key elements to emphasize:

Privacy and Confidentiality: Begin by stating that the conversation is private and will be kept confidential, within legal and organizational limits. "Before we start, I want to assure you that this conversation is confidential, and anything we discuss will stay between us unless there's a safety concern or a legal requirement to share."

Focus on Behavior, Not Judgment: Describe what you see *or* hear, *not what you* think is happening. Avoid words like "lazy," "unmotivated," or "difficult." Instead, use objective observations like "quieter," "less engaged," or "missed deadlines."

Express Genuine Care: Frame the conversation around your concern for their well-being. Use phrases like "I'm concerned," "I want to check in," or "I want to make sure you're okay."

Open-Ended Questions: Encourage them to share by asking open-ended questions. "How are things with you at the moment?" "Is there anything going on that's making work feel particularly challenging?"

Script Example 2: Addressing a Specific Work Impact with a Well-being Focus

"Hi [Employee Name], thanks for meeting with me. I wanted to touch base about [specific project or task]. I've noticed that [describe the specific work impact, e.g., the recent report wasn't submitted on time, or there were a few errors in the client proposal]. I know this isn't typical for you, and I wanted to check in to see if there's anything affecting your ability to focus or manage your workload at the moment. My priority is to ensure everyone on the team is well and has the resources they need. How are you feeling about your work and your capacity right now?"

Key elements to emphasize:

Connect Work to Well-being: Link observable work performance issues directly to your concern for their overall well-being, rather than simply issuing a performance critique.

Acknowledge Their Usual Performance: Acknowledging their usual high performance can soften the impact of discussing a current performance dip and signal that you recognize their capabilities.

Offer Support Proactively: Make it clear that you are there to help find solutions.

Offering Support and Guiding Towards Resources

Once an employee begins to feel comfortable and ready to hear, or even if they initially deflect, your role is to listen actively, empathize, and gently guide them toward appropriate support. It's vital to remember that you are not a therapist, but a supportive colleague and leader. Your primary responsibility is to connect them with the right resources.

Listening Actively and Empathizing:

Use Verbal and Non-Verbal Cues: Nod, maintain eye contact (if comfortable for both parties), and use affirmations like "I hear you," "That sounds difficult," or "I understand."

Paraphrase and Summarize: To ensure you've understood correctly and to show you're listening, remember what they've said. "So, if I'm understanding correctly, you're feeling overwhelmed by the workload, and that's making it hard to concentrate. Is that right?"

Validate Their Feelings: Acknowledge that their feelings are valid, even if you don't fully understand the situation. "It's completely understandable that you'd feel that way given what you're going through."

Offering Support and Identifying Resources:

Script Example 3: Offering Direct Support and Information about Resources

"Thank you for sharing that with me, [Employee Name]. I really appreciate the fact that you are openly talking to me. It sounds like you're going through a lot right now, and I want to reiterate that your well-being is important to us. We have several resources available that might be helpful. Our Employee Assistance Program (EAP) offers confidential counseling services with trained professionals, and it's available 24/7. I can provide you with the contact details and a brochure if you'd like. Additionally, we can explore options like adjusting your workload temporarily, or if you feel you need some time to focus on yourself, we can discuss taking some personal leave or sick leave. What feels like the most helpful step for you right now?"

Key elements to emphasize:

Acknowledge and Validate: "Thank you for sharing. It sounds like you're dealing with a lot."

Reiterate Support: "We're here to support you."

Introduce Specific Resources: Mention the EAP, HR department, or any other relevant internal or external support systems. Be prepared to provide contact information and a brief explanation of what each resource offers.

Offer Practical Work Adjustments: Discuss potential immediate workplace adjustments such as flexible hours, temporary task reallocation, or reduced responsibilities, if appropriate and feasible.

Discuss Leave Options: If personal time off seems appropriate, discuss the options available, such as sick leave, personal leave, or disability leave, and explain the process clearly and empathetically.

Empower the Employee: Ask them what they feel would be most helpful. This gives them a sense of control and agency in their own recovery and support process.

Script Example 4: When an Employee is Unsure About Seeking Help

"I understand that reaching out for professional help can feel like a big step, [Employee Name]. Sometimes just talking about it can be a good start, and I'm here to listen. When you feel ready, the EAP is a good option because it's completely confidential and the counselors are experts in helping people navigate these kinds of challenges. There's no pressure at all, but I want you to know if the option is there. Would it be helpful if I just sent you the information for the EAP, so you have it handy with no strings attached? We can also talk about what a smaller step might look like, perhaps just discussing how we can better manage your workload in the immediate term."

Key elements to emphasize:

Acknowledge Hesitation: "I understand that reaching out can feel like a big step."

Reiterate Confidentiality and Expertise: Remind them of the benefits of professional support.

No Pressure Approach: Make it clear that the decision to use resources is theirs.

Offer Immediate, Smaller Steps: Suggest practical, immediate work-related support as a stepping stone.

Discussing Time-Off Requests with Support and Understanding

Beyond direct mental health crises, fostering a supportive environment also means approaching requests for time off, whether for mental health reasons or otherwise, with genuine understanding and a focus on employee well-being. The goal is to take time to recharge and to make the process as smooth and supportive as possible.

Script Example 5: Responding to a Mental Health-Related Leave Request

"Thank you for coming to me with this, [Employee Name]. I understand you need to take some time off to focus on your mental well-being, and I fully support that. Your health is the priority. We can arrange for you to take [mention type of leave, e.g., sick leave, personal leave] starting [proposed start date]. Please work with HR to complete the necessary paperwork. I want to make sure your transition back to work is as smooth as possible. When you feel up to it, we can discuss how to manage your workload and hand over your responsibilities before you go, and plan for your return. In the meantime, please focus on your recovery. Is there anything you need immediately from me before you start your leave?"

Key elements to emphasize:

Direct Support and Validation: "I fully support your taking time for your mental well-being."

Clarify Leave Type and Process: Clearly state the type of leave being approved and guide them to HR for procedural details.

Focus on Transition and Return: Proactively think about the practicalities of their absence and return to ease their burden.

Encourage Focus on Recovery: Explicitly tell them to prioritize their health.

Offer Immediate Assistance: Ask what they need before they leave.

Script Example 6: Responding to a General Time-Off Request (Vacation, Personal Days)

"Hi [Employee Name], thanks for submitting your request for time off from [Start Date] to [End Date]. I've reviewed it and it's approved. I'm glad you're taking some time to recharge. Please ensure your key responsibilities are covered and any urgent tasks are handed over to [Colleague Name] or completed before you leave. Let me know if there's anything I can do to help with the handover. Enjoy your time off, and we look forward to having you back refreshed."

Key elements to emphasize:

Clear Approval: Provide definitive approval.

Positive Reinforcement: Frame taking time off as a positive and necessary action. "I'm glad you're taking time to recharge."

Practical Handover Guidance: Offer brief, clear instructions for managing work coverage.

Positive Closing: Wish them a good break.

Key Principles for All Difficult and Supportive Dialogues:

1. **Confidentiality is Paramount:** Always respect an employee's privacy. Only share information on a need-to-know basis with HR or other relevant parties, and always with the employee's consent

where possible, or as dictated by legal or ethical obligations.

2. **Listen More Than You Speak:** Give the employee ample opportunity to express themselves without interruption.
3. **Be Present and Attentive:** Put away distractions, focus on the individual, and demonstrate that you are fully engaged in the conversation.
4. **Avoid Making Assumptions or Diagnoses:** You are not a clinician. Your role is to support, listen, and provide guidance, including helping find professional resources. Phrases like "It sounds like you might be experiencing burnout" are best avoided; instead, focus on observed behaviors and offer support.
5. **Know Your Resources:** Be familiar with your organization's EAP, HR policies, and any other mental health support services available.
6. **Document Conversations:** Keep brief, factual notes of conversations, especially those involving performance issues or discussions about support and resources. This is important for organizational record-keeping and can be a safeguard.
7. **Follow Up:** Check in with the employee after a period to see how they are doing and if the support they receive has been helpful. This reinforces your ongoing commitment to their well-being.
8. **Self-Care for Leaders:** These conversations can be emotionally taxing. Ensure you also have your own support system and practice self-care.

By preparing with these scripts and internalizing the underlying principles, leaders and HR professionals can approach sensitive conversations with greater confidence, fostering a workplace culture where mental health is prioritized, and employees feel genuinely supported. These dialogues are not just about managing immediate issues; they are foundational to building trust, psychological safety, and a resilient workforce.

Policies for Equal Treatment of Mental Health Absences

The bedrock of a truly supportive workplace lies in the equitable treatment of all employee absences, irrespective of their underlying cause. Historically, and regrettably, mental health-related absences have often been subject to greater scrutiny, stigma, and differential treatment compared to those stemming from physical ailments. This disparity not only undermines employee well-being but also creates a culture of fear and silence, discouraging individuals from seeking necessary support. To foster genuine psychological safety and a robust, resilient workforce, it is imperative to embed policies that explicitly grant mental health absences the same parity and understanding as physical health absences. This involves a multi-faceted approach to policy development and implementation, ensuring that the organizational framework actively champions inclusivity and support.

Developing or updating Human Resources policies to reflect this principle of equal treatment is a critical first step. Such policies should clearly articulate that periods of absence due to mental health conditions are legitimate and will be managed with the same degree of care, confidentiality, and support as absences due to physical illness. This means moving away from implicit hierarchies where a broken limb is seen as more valid than a period of debilitating anxiety or depression. The language within these policies is paramount. It should be inclusive, empathetic, and devoid of any judgment. Phrases like "mental health day," while sometimes used colloquially, can inadvertently reinforce the idea that these are discretionary or less serious than other forms of leave. Instead, policies should refer to "sick leave," "personal leave," or "medical leave" that encompasses both physical and mental health needs.

A key component of this policy framework is the establishment of clear, accessible, and confidential procedures for reporting mental health-related absences. Employees should not feel they need to over-explain or justify their need for leave due to a mental health condition. The process should mirror that for physical health absences: a straightforward notification to a manager or HR department, with appropriate documentation if required by law or company policy, but without demanding sensitive personal details up front unless necessary for medical certification or accommodation discussions. For instance, a policy might state: "Employees requiring time off due to illness, whether physical or mental, should notify their manager or HR by [method of notification] within [timeframe]. Medical certification may be required by the company or statutory bodies to support longer periods of absence or to facilitate appropriate accommodations." This ensures consistency and removes the burden of selective disclosure from the employee.

Furthermore, the return-to-work process following a mental health absence requires careful consideration and planning. Just as an employee recovering from surgery would benefit from a phased return or adjusted duties, individuals returning from mental health leave may need similar accommodations. Policies should outline provisions for return-to-work plans, which might include gradual reintegration into the workplace, flexible working arrangements, temporary adjustments to workload, or modified tasks. These plans should be developed collaboratively between the employee, their manager, and HR, with input from healthcare professionals if available and consented to by the employee. The aim is to support a smooth and sustainable return, preventing premature relapse and reinforcing the employees' value to the organization. For example, a policy might include a clause such as: "Upon return from a period of medical leave related to mental health, employees may be eligible for a phased return-to-work program, subject to medical advice and operational feasibility. This may involve adjustments to working hours, duties, or the work environment to support a successful reintegration."

Protecting employees from stigma or discrimination is intrinsically linked to the equal treatment of mental health absences. Policies must explicitly prohibit any form of discrimination or reprisal against employees who take time off for mental health reasons. This includes ensuring that such absences do not negatively impact performance reviews, promotion opportunities, or job security. Organizational culture plays a vital role here, and policies should be supported by training managers and staff on mental health awareness, unconscious bias, and the importance of creating an inclusive environment. Clear channels for reporting any perceived discrimination or stigma should also be established, with robust investigation procedures in place. This might be framed within a broader anti-discrimination policy, with a specific addendum addressing mental health. For instance, "The organization is committed to fostering a workplace free from discrimination and stigma. All employees are protected from reprisal or adverse action because of taking approved medical leave, including leave for mental health reasons. Any employee who believes they have experienced discrimination or reprisal should report it to HR for investigation."

Compliance with relevant legislation is a non-negotiable aspect of policy development. Depending on the jurisdiction, various laws may govern employee rights related to sick leave, disability, and mental health. For example, the Americans with Disabilities Act (ADA) in the United States requires employers to provide reasonable accommodations for employees with disabilities, which can include mental health conditions. Similarly, laws in other countries often mandate paid sick leave and prohibit discrimination based on health status. Organizations must ensure their policies not only meet but exceed these legal minimums, aligning with best practices in workplace mental health support. This requires ongoing monitoring of legislative changes and consulting with legal counsel to ensure compliance. A policy might include a statement like: "This policy is implemented in accordance with all applicable federal, state, and local laws regarding employee leave and disability. Employees are encouraged to consult with HR for specific information regarding their rights and entitlements."

Creating an inclusive and supportive framework that encourages employees to take necessary time off without fear of reprisal is the ultimate goal. This goes beyond mere policy statements and requires a cultural shift. When employees feel psychologically safe, they are more likely to be open about their needs and utilize available support systems. This can be fostered through various means, including:

Leadership Buy-in and Role Modeling: Senior leaders demonstrating their commitment to mental health by openly discussing its importance, sharing personal experiences (where appropriate and comfortable), and visibly supporting mental health initiatives can have a profound impact. When leaders prioritize their own well-being and openly discuss taking time off to rest and recharge, it signals to the rest of the organization that this is acceptable and encouraged.

Mental Health Training for All Employees: Providing training that educates all employees about mental health, destigmatizes mental illness, and equips them with basic skills to support colleagues can create a more empathetic and understanding workplace. This training should cover recognizing signs of distress, having supportive conversations, and knowing where to direct individuals for help, aligning with the principles discussed in the previous sections.

Promoting Employee Assistance Programs (EAPs) and Other Resources: Organizations should actively and consistently promote the availability of EAPs, mental health benefits, and other support services. This includes making information easily accessible, clearly explaining the confidential nature of these services, and normalizing their use. Regular communication campaigns can reinforce their value.

Flexible Work Arrangements: Beyond return-to-work plans, offering ongoing flexibility in work arrangements, such as remote work options, adjusted hours, or compressed workweeks, can significantly support employees in managing their mental well-being and preventing burnout. These arrangements can be particularly beneficial for individuals managing chronic mental health conditions.

Regular Check-ins and Open Communication: Managers should be trained to conduct regular, informal check-ins with their team members, focusing on well-being as much as work progress. These check-ins can create an environment where employees feel comfortable raising concerns before they escalate. The conversational frameworks provided earlier are crucial tools for these interactions.

Reviewing and Updating Policies Regularly: The landscape of mental health and workplace support is continually evolving. Organizations should periodically review their policies, incorporating feedback from employees and staying abreast of best practices and legislative changes to ensure their framework remains relevant and effective.

By implementing these comprehensive policies and fostering a supportive culture, organizations can move towards a reality where mental health absences are not viewed as a liability or a source of stigma, but as a necessary component of overall employee health and a signal that the organization prioritizes the holistic well-being of its people. This commitment not only benefits individual employees but also contributes to a more engaged, productive, and resilient workforce, ultimately strengthening the organization as a whole. The transition from viewing mental health as a secondary concern to an integral part of operational health requires deliberate, consistent, and empathetic policy creation and application. This section underscores the practical steps involved in ensuring that the policies in place actively dismantle stigma and create a safety net for all employees, promoting an environment where taking care of one's mental health is a recognized and supported aspect of professional life.

The practical implementation of policies ensuring equal treatment of mental health absences involves several key considerations, extending beyond the initial drafting and communication. One critical area is the management of medical documentation. While it is essential to respect employee privacy, employers also have legitimate needs for information to manage absences, process benefits, and ensure compliance with legal requirements. Policies should therefore strike a balance. They should specify what type of documentation is acceptable for supporting a leave request related to mental health, without requiring an explicit diagnosis to be shared with the immediate manager. For instance, a doctor's note could state that the employee is under their care and requires a period of absence from work, or that specific accommodations are recommended, without detailing the nature of the mental health condition. The responsibility for managing more sensitive medical information should be with a designated HR professional or a third-party administrator, ensuring a higher level of confidentiality and expertise in handling such matters. This approach respects the employee's privacy while allowing the organization to manage absences effectively and legally.

Another important aspect is the consistent application of policies. Discrepancies in how mental health absences are handled across different departments or by different managers can quickly erode trust and create perceptions of unfairness.

Therefore, robust training for all managers is crucial. This training should cover not only the 'what' and 'why' of the policies but also the 'how' – providing them with the skills and confidence to manage these situations empathetically and effectively, as discussed in previous sections. Regular refreshers and updates are also advisable to ensure ongoing understanding and compliance. When managers are equipped to handle these conversations and administrative processes with sensitivity and fairness, it significantly contributes to the overall positive impact of the policies.

The interaction between mental health policies and other HR frameworks, such as performance management, disciplinary procedures, and compensation, also needs careful alignment. For example, an employee experiencing a mental health crisis and needing to take leave should not face punitive measures for performance dips that occur during this period, provided they follow the correct notification and documentation procedures. Similarly, if an employee is struggling with a mental health condition that impacts their work, the first step should be to explore support and accommodations, rather than immediately initiating disciplinary action. Policies must clearly delineate that legitimate, supported absences due to mental health should not be conflated with performance issues that require disciplinary intervention. This alignment ensures that the organization's various HR practices are mutually reinforcing and supportive of employee well-being.

Furthermore, the role of supervisors and team leaders in fostering a supportive environment for mental health absences cannot be overstated. While policies provide the framework, it is the day-to-day interactions and the team culture that truly determine whether these policies are effective. Encouraging open dialogue about stress and workload, promoting work-life balance, and ensuring that colleagues are respectful and supportive of those who need to take time off are all critical. Leaders can model healthy behaviors, such as taking breaks and using vacation time, and actively discourage presenteeism – the act of coming to work while sick or unwell, which can be particularly detrimental when dealing with mental health challenges. Creating a culture where taking a mental health day is as normalized as taking a day off for a physical illness requires consistent effort and reinforcement from leadership at all levels.

It is also beneficial for organizations to consider the broader ecosystem of mental health support, which includes how absences are integrated with benefits like short-term disability (STD) or long-term disability (LTD) plans, where applicable. Policies should clearly outline the process for applying for these benefits, ensuring that employees understand the eligibility criteria and the documentation required. A smooth and transparent process for accessing disability benefits can be a vital safety net for employees experiencing significant mental health challenges that prevent them from working for extended periods. This requires close coordination between HR, benefit providers, and the employee, ensuring that the process itself does not become a source of undue stress.

Moreover, organizations should be mindful of the potential for unintended consequences when developing policies. For example, overly strict documentation requirements or a lack of clarity around the process can inadvertently deter employees from taking needed leave. Conversely, policies that are too lenient without adequate support structures in place could potentially be exploited, though this is far less common than the issue of underutilization of leave. The focus should always be on creating a policy that is supportive, clear, fair, and compliant, with built-in mechanisms for review and improvement. Employee feedback mechanisms, such as anonymous surveys or focus groups, can be invaluable in identifying areas where policies might be falling short or could be enhanced.

In conclusion, the establishment of policies for the equal treatment of mental health absences is not merely a procedural requirement; it is a fundamental ethical and strategic imperative. It signifies an organization's commitment to the holistic well-being of its employees, fostering an environment of trust, psychological safety, and mutual respect. By ensuring that mental health is treated with the same importance as physical health in all aspects of absence management, from reporting and documentation to return-to-work processes and protection against discrimination, organizations can build a more resilient, engaged, and ultimately, more successful workforce. These policies serve as a tangible demonstration of an organization's values and its understanding that the health of its people is inextricably linked to the health of the business.

Chapter 9
Cultivating Focus without Meetings

The relentless hum of notifications, the constant ping of instant messages, and the ever-present calendar dotted with back-to-back meetings – this is the modern workplace reality for many. This environment, while seemingly efficient, often fragments attention, stifles deep thinking, and contributes significantly to employee stress and burnout. To counteract this, organizations are increasingly exploring and implementing "meeting-free" blocks or days. These dedicated periods are designed to reclaim focus, enable concentrated work, and ultimately foster a more sustainable and less draining work environment. This subsection delves into the practical strategies for successfully integrating these blocks into the organizational fabric, ensuring they deliver on their promise of enhanced productivity and reduced stress.

The journey towards implementing meeting-free blocks begins with a clear understanding of their purpose and the benefits they offer. Unlike simply reducing the number of meetings, these blocks are intentionally carved out from the typical schedule to facilitate what is often referred to as "deep work" – tasks requiring sustained concentration and cognitive effort, such as strategic planning, complex problem-solving, coding, writing, or creative ideation. By eliminating the interruption of meetings, employees are empowered to engage in these critical activities without the cognitive overhead of context-switching. This not only leads to higher quality output but also provides a sense of accomplishment and control, which are potent antidotes to workplace stress. Furthermore, these blocks can serve as a collective sigh of relief, signaling to employees that their focused work is valued and that the organization recognizes the detrimental impact of constant interruptions.

The practical implementation of meeting-free blocks requires a structured and deliberate approach. The first crucial step is to define the scope and frequency of these blocks. Will they be daily occurrences, perhaps a dedicated morning or afternoon each week? Or will they be a full day once a month? The decision should be guided by the nature of the work performed within the organization and the existing meeting culture. For some, a daily protected focus time of two to three hours might be sufficient. For others, a full "no-meeting day" once a week or bi-weekly could be more effective. It's important to start with a pilot program to gauge effectiveness and gather feedback before a company-wide rollout. This iterative approach allows for adjustments based on real-world experience, ensuring the chosen structure aligns with the organization's operational needs.

Once the framework is established, clear communication is paramount. Employees need to understand *why* these blocks are being implemented, what is expected of them during these times, and how the organization will support this new practice. This communication should come from leadership, reinforcing the strategic importance of focused work and employee well-being. Explaining that these blocks are not about avoiding collaboration but about optimizing individual and team productivity can help manage initial skepticism. A clear policy or guideline document should be created, outlining the designated meeting-free times, the types of activities that are encouraged during these periods, and crucially, what constitutes an exception. Exceptions should be rare and rigorously justified, perhaps for critical client emergencies or pre-scheduled, high-stakes external meetings that cannot be moved.

Gaining buy-in from various stakeholders, particularly middle management and team leaders, is another critical element. They are often the gatekeepers of team schedules and can either champion or inadvertently undermine the initiative. Engaging them in the planning process, soliciting their input on the best times and formats for meeting-free blocks, and equipping them with the skills to manage their teams' schedules effectively will be key. This might involve training on how to decline or reschedule non-essential meetings that encroach upon these blocks, and how to communicate the importance of this focused time to their teams. Leaders should also model the behavior themselves, visibly adhering to the meeting-free blocks and encouraging their teams to do the same.

Managing potential pushbacks requires a proactive and empathetic approach. Some employees might express concerns about falling behind on collaborative tasks or worry that essential discussions will be missed. It's important to acknowledge these concerns and offer solutions. For instance, establishing clear protocols for urgent communications that might arise during a meeting-free block – perhaps a designated emergency contact or a specific channel for critical issues – can alleviate anxiety. The policy should also specify that while internal meetings are discouraged, essential external client meetings or critical operational discussions may still be necessary. Still, these should be the exception and require careful consideration and justification. The emphasis should be on creating protected time for deep work, not on eliminating all forms of communication or collaboration.

Integrating meeting-free blocks into existing workflows necessitates a conscious effort to shift ingrained habits. This often involves a cultural change, where the default assumption moves from constant availability and immediate responsiveness to prioritizing focused work. Calendar blocking is a fundamental tool. Employees and teams should be encouraged to block out these periods on their shared calendars, clearly marking them as "Focus Time" or "Deep Work." This visual cue serves as a constant reminder and discourages others from scheduling meetings during these times. Furthermore, leveraging technology can be beneficial. Many calendar applications allow for the designation of "busy" or "free" statuses, and setting these blocks can signal availability to colleagues. Some organizations even implement "focus modes" on communication platforms, which can automatically mute notifications and display a status indicating that an employee is engaged in focused work.

The success of meeting-free blocks also hinges on establishing clear expectations about what constitutes appropriate use of this time. Employees should be encouraged to proactively plan their focused work during these periods, identifying specific tasks they aim to accomplish. This might involve blocking out specific time slots for particular projects or dedicating entire blocks to a single, complex task. Managers can play a role in facilitating this by helping their team members prioritize and allocate their focus time effectively. For example, during a team meeting at the beginning of the week, the discussion could include which projects or tasks warrant dedicated focus time in the upcoming week. This proactive planning ensures that the time is used purposefully and contributes to tangible progress.

Furthermore, the policy around meeting-free blocks should address the concept of "availability." While the intent is to reduce internal meeting interruptions, it doesn't mean employees are entirely inaccessible for urgent matters. The policy should define what constitutes an urgent matter and establish clear channels for addressing such situations. This might involve a dedicated urgent communication channel, or a protocol for contacting a colleague or manager directly if a situation cannot wait. The key is to create a system that allows for essential urgent communications without undermining the integrity of the protected focus time. This requires a delicate balance, ensuring that the focus blocks are respected as a priority for deep work, while still maintaining operational responsiveness.

Another important aspect to consider is the potential for these blocks to become a new source of stress if not managed effectively. If employees feel pressured to cram an unmanageable amount of work into these limited focus periods, or if they are constantly interrupted despite the policy, the intended benefits can be negated. Therefore, it is crucial to monitor the effectiveness of these blocks, gather feedback from employees, and adjust as needed. This might involve refining the timing or duration of the blocks, providing additional training on time management and prioritization, or reinforcing the policy with those who consistently disregard it. A flexible and adaptable approach is essential for long-term success.

To truly embed meeting-free blocks into the organizational culture, it's important to celebrate and acknowledge the positive outcomes. Sharing success stories and highlighting how these blocks have enabled significant progress on key projects can reinforce their value and encourage continued adherence. This could involve internal communications, team huddles, or even informal recognition of individuals or teams who have effectively utilized their focus time. When employees see tangible benefits and feel that their well-being and productivity are genuinely being prioritized, they are more likely to embrace and champion this new way of working.

The implementation of meeting-free blocks is not a one-time event but an ongoing process of refinement and cultural adaptation. It requires commitment from leadership, active participation from employees, and a willingness to experiment and learn. By carefully planning, communicating clearly, managing expectations, and continuously seeking feedback, organizations can successfully create dedicated time for focused work, leading to reduced stress, enhanced productivity, and a healthier, more sustainable work environment for everyone. This proactive approach to managing the demands of modern work is not just a productivity hack; it's a strategic investment in the well-being and effectiveness of the workforce. It acknowledges that sustained, deep concentration is a critical component of innovation and high-quality output, and that deliberately protecting this capacity is a hallmark of a forward-thinking and supportive organization. The shift requires a conscious effort to redefine what "being productive" looks like, moving away from a culture that often equates busyness with effectiveness, towards one that values focused, high-impact work.

In the intricate ecosystem of the modern workplace, where the demands for productivity often compete with the imperative of employee well-being, fostering a sense of autonomy emerges as a cornerstone of sustainable engagement and robust resilience. Autonomy, at its core, is freedom and capacity for self-governance, the ability to direct one's own actions and make choices regarding one's work. When employees experience a genuine sense of autonomy, they are not merely cogs in a machine, but active participants who feel a profound connection to their roles and a vested interest in the success of their endeavors. This intrinsic motivation, fueled by the power of choice and self-direction, is a potent antidote to the disengagement and burnout that plague many organizations today.

The direct correlation between autonomy and employee engagement is well-documented. When individuals are empowered to make decisions about their tasks, workflows, and even the timing and location of their work, they develop a stronger sense of ownership. This ownership translates into a deeper commitment to the quality of their output, as they feel directly responsible for the outcomes of their choices. This is in stark contrast to environments where work is rigidly dictated, leaving employees feeling like passive executors of directives. In such scenarios, the connection to the work itself can become tenuous, leading to a decline in motivation and a heightened susceptibility to stress. By providing avenues for self-determination, leaders cultivate an environment where employees are more likely to invest their energy, creativity, and best efforts. This proactive involvement naturally enhances their overall engagement levels, as they perceive their contributions as meaningful and valued.

Moreover, autonomy is intrinsically linked to mental resilience. The ability to navigate challenges, adapt to change, and bounce back from setbacks is significantly bolstered when individuals feel they have a degree of control over their circumstances. In a work context, this translates to the freedom to problem-solve, to experiment with different approaches, and to learn from mistakes without the paralyzing fear of reprisal. When employees are trusted to manage their own processes and make decisions within defined parameters, they build confidence in their abilities. This self-efficacy, the belief in one's capacity to succeed, is a powerful buffer against stress and a critical component of psychological well-being. Conversely, a lack of autonomy can foster feelings of helplessness and powerlessness, making individuals more vulnerable to the corrosive effects of workplace stressors and increasing the likelihood of mental fatigue and eventual burnout.

Effective delegation is a foundational strategy for cultivating autonomy. It moves beyond simply assigning tasks; it involves entrusting individuals with the responsibility and authority to see those tasks through to completion. This requires a shift in leadership mindset, from one of close supervision to one of empowered oversight. Leaders must be willing to relinquish a degree of control, recognizing that their team members possess the skills and capabilities to excel. The process begins with clearly defining the desired outcome and the scope of the delegated task. However, instead of dictating the precise steps to be taken, leaders should encourage the employee to propose their own approach. This collaborative process of defining the "what" while allowing the employee to determine the "how" is a powerful way to foster autonomy and build trust. It signals a belief in their competence and provides an opportunity for them to apply their unique skills and perspectives.

Trust is the bedrock upon which autonomy is built. Leaders must cultivate a culture of psychological safety where employees feel safe to take calculated risks, to voice opinions, and to learn from errors. This trust is earned through consistent behavior, transparency, and a genuine commitment to employee development. When leaders demonstrate that they trust their teams, they empower them to take ownership and to make decisions independently. This doesn't mean a complete absence of guidance or support. Rather, it means providing the necessary resources, information, and occasional checkpoints to ensure alignment and address any emerging challenges. It's about enabling the employee to navigate their work with confidence, knowing that they have the backing of their leadership. This trust-building exercise is a continuous process, reinforcing the understanding that each team member is a valued contributor with the capacity for independent thought and action.

Empowering individuals to make decisions related to their work is a tangible manifestation of fostering autonomy. This can take many forms, from allowing employees to choose the order in which they tackle their assignments to involving them in project planning and problem-solving sessions. For instance, a project manager might delegate a significant component of a new initiative to a team member, not only by assigning the task but also by granting them the authority to select the methodologies, tools, and even the specific team members they will collaborate with, within predefined constraints. This level of decision-making power imbues the employee with a profound sense of agency and responsibility. They become invested in the success of the project not just because it's their job, but because they have had a hand in shaping its trajectory. This sense of ownership naturally drives higher levels of engagement and a greater willingness to go the extra mile.

Flexibility in how, when, and where work is done is a significant contributor to a sense of control and a powerful stress reducer. The traditional nine-to-five, in-office model, while historically prevalent, does not cater to the diverse needs and preferences of today's workforce. Offering options such as remote work, hybrid arrangements, flexible scheduling, or compressed workweeks allows employees to tailor their work lives to better accommodate personal responsibilities, optimize their energy levels, and create a more harmonious work-life integration. When an employee has the flexibility to choose when they are most productive, or to work from a location that minimizes distractions and personal stress, they experience a heightened sense of autonomy. This control over their work environment and schedule can significantly reduce feelings of being overwhelmed and can foster a greater sense of well-being. It acknowledges that individual circumstances vary and that a one-size-fits-all approach to work is often counterproductive.

Consider an employee who thrives in the early morning hours, completing their most demanding tasks before the typical workday even begins. Offering them the flexibility to adjust their start and end times, perhaps coming in later if they have a late-evening personal commitment, allows them to capitalize on their peak productivity window. This flexibility not only enhances their output but also demonstrates that the organization values their individual working style and well-being. Similarly, allowing team members to work remotely on certain days can reduce commute stress, save time, and enable them to create a personalized workspace that fosters focus. The key is to establish clear expectations regarding communication, availability, and performance metrics, ensuring that flexibility does not equate to a lack of accountability. When implemented thoughtfully, this flexibility becomes a powerful tool for fostering autonomy and enhancing job satisfaction.

The ripple effect of fostering autonomy is evident in increased job satisfaction and a heightened sense of creativity. When employees have the freedom to innovate, to experiment, and to approach their work in ways that align with their strengths and interests, their jobs become more stimulating and fulfilling. This intrinsic reward system is far more sustainable and powerful than external motivators alone. A team member who is empowered to research and propose new solutions to a recurring problem, for instance, is more likely to be engaged in the process and proud of the outcome, regardless of whether the solution is ultimately adopted. This proactive engagement in problem-solving and idea generation not only benefits the individual but also drives innovation within the organization. It taps into the collective intelligence of the workforce, unlocking potential that might otherwise remain dormant.

Furthermore, autonomy fosters a stronger sense of ownership and accountability. When individuals are given the freedom to make choices and are entrusted with responsibilities, they naturally feel a greater sense of ownership over their work and its results. This ownership is not merely about personal pride; it's about a deeper understanding of their role in the larger organizational picture. They are more likely to take initiative, to be proactive in identifying and addressing potential issues, and to hold themselves accountable for delivering high-quality outcomes. This contrasts sharply with environments where employees may feel like they are merely executing tasks assigned to them, with little personal stake in the ultimate success or failure. The empowered employee, feeling a sense of control and agency, becomes a more responsible and accountable contributor.

To effectively implement strategies that foster autonomy, leaders must actively practice principles of effective delegation. This involves identifying tasks that are suitable for delegation, considering the skills and development needs of their team members. It's not about offloading undesirable work but about providing opportunities for growth and demonstrating trust. For example, instead of simply telling a junior team member to "handle client inquiries," a leader might delegate the responsibility of managing a specific client relationship. This would involve providing the necessary training, resources, and ongoing support, while empowering the junior member to be the primary point of contact, managing communication, and resolving issues independently. This type of delegation fosters a deeper sense of responsibility and allows the individual to develop critical client management skills.

A crucial element in empowering employees is to establish clear boundaries and expectations. While autonomy is about freedom, it is not about anarchy. Leaders must provide a framework within which autonomy can flourish. This includes defining performance standards, outlining ethical guidelines, and communicating the organization's strategic objectives. By setting these parameters, leaders ensure that employees' independent actions are aligned with the broader organizational goals. For instance, a software development team might be given the autonomy to choose their development methodologies and tools. Still, they must adhere to the company's cybersecurity protocols and deliver code that meets specific quality assurance standards. This balance between freedom and structure ensures that autonomy is a catalyst for productive and responsible action, rather than a recipe for chaos.

The act of trusting employees is a powerful motivator. When leaders consistently demonstrate faith in their team's capabilities, it creates a virtuous cycle. Employees who feel trusted are more likely to be motivated to live up to that trust, leading to increased engagement and improved performance. This trust can be demonstrated through various actions, such as allowing employees to manage their own schedules, empowering them to make decisions on project approaches, or refraining from micromanaging their daily activities. For example, a manager might trust their sales team to set their own outreach strategies and manage their client interactions, providing support and guidance as needed but allowing the team to take ownership of their targets and methods. This level of trust signals a profound respect for the team's expertise and judgment.

The tangible impact of this empowerment is often seen in increased innovation and creativity. When employees are not constrained by rigid processes and are encouraged to explore new ideas, they are more likely to develop novel solutions and approaches. A marketing team, for instance, might be given the autonomy to experiment with different social media campaigns, allowing them to test new platforms or creative content formats. The understanding is that not every experiment will yield immediate success, but the learning derived from these initiatives is invaluable. This willingness to embrace experimentation, fostered by a culture of autonomy, is what drives genuine innovation and allows organizations to stay ahead in competitive landscapes. It encourages a mindset of continuous improvement and adaptability.

Furthermore, autonomy cultivates a greater sense of accountability. When individuals feel they have a genuine stake in their work, they are more inclined to take responsibility for its success. This means being proactive in identifying potential roadblocks, seeking out necessary information, and owning the outcomes of their decisions. Instead of waiting for instructions, empowered employees take initiative. For example, if a team member identifies a potential efficiency improvement in a workflow, their sense of autonomy would likely drive them to research the change, propose it to their manager, and perhaps even lead to its implementation. This level of proactive engagement and self-direction is a hallmark of a highly accountable and engaged workforce. It signifies a shift from being a recipient of work to being a proprietor of it.

To foster autonomy effectively, leaders should regularly solicit feedback from their teams regarding their needs and preferences. This could involve one-on-one discussions, team meetings, or anonymous surveys. Understanding what aspects of their work employees feel they lack control over, or where they would benefit from more decision-making power, is crucial for tailoring support. For instance, a team might express a desire for more input into project timelines or a greater say in the tools they use for collaboration. By actively listening to this feedback and making demonstrable efforts to address it, leaders not only empower their teams but also build stronger relationships based on mutual respect and understanding. This continuous dialogue ensures that the organization's approach to fostering autonomy remains relevant and impactful.

Ultimately, the cultivation of autonomy is not merely a management technique; it is a strategic imperative for building a thriving, engaged, and resilient workforce. By entrusting employees with decision-making power, providing flexibility, and fostering a culture of trust and accountability, leaders can unlock the full potential of their teams. This commitment to empowering individuals not only enhances job satisfaction and boosts productivity but also equips employees with the psychological resources necessary to navigate the inherent challenges of the modern workplace, paving the way for sustained success and well-being. It is an investment in human capital that yields significant returns, creating an environment where individuals feel valued, capable, and motivated to contribute their best, day in and day out.

In the landscape of professional development, the art of feedback stands as a critical juncture where potential meets performance. It is through considered, growth-oriented feedback that individuals are guided, encouraged, and equipped to navigate their professional journeys with increasing skill and confidence. This is not about identifying flaws or assigning blame; rather, it is about illuminating pathways for enhancement, recognizing achievements, and fostering an environment where continuous learning is not just expected but actively celebrated. When feedback is delivered with an intent to develop, it transforms from a potentially daunting review into a powerful catalyst for personal and professional evolution. It reinforces the notion that every individual within an organization is on a path of continuous growth, a journey supported by insightful guidance and positive reinforcement.

The foundational principle of growth-oriented feedback lies in its specificity and actionability. Vague pronouncements, such as "do better" or "needs improvement," offer little to no clarity for the recipient. Instead, effective feedback focuses on concrete behaviors, observable actions, and specific outcomes. For example, instead of telling a team member that their presentation was "unclear," a growth-oriented approach would involve pinpointing specific slides or segments that lacked clarity, perhaps suggesting the use of more visual aids or a clearer explanation of complex data points. This level of detail empowers the individual to understand precisely what needs adjustment. It shifts the focus from a general sense of inadequacy to a targeted area for improvement, making the feedback actionable. When feedback is tied to observable actions, it becomes a diagnostic tool, allowing the employee to understand the 'why' behind the suggested changes and to apply them effectively in future endeavors. This precision is paramount in ensuring that feedback is received as helpful guidance rather than an indictment.

Furthermore, the delivery of feedback should always be framed with a positive and supportive intent, even when addressing areas that require development. This involves acknowledging the individual's efforts, recognizing their strengths, and framing suggestions for improvement as opportunities for learning and skill enhancement. For instance, when providing feedback on a report that requires more in-depth analysis, a manager might begin by commending the employee for the thoroughness of the data collection and the clarity of the initial findings. The feedback on the analytical depth can then be presented as a way to "further strengthen your insights" or "add another layer of valuable analysis to your already robust work." This approach helps to mitigate defensiveness and encourages the employee to engage with the feedback constructively. By emphasizing the positive and the potential, feedback becomes an invitation to grow, rather than a criticism of current performance. This framing is crucial for building psychological safety, where individuals feel comfortable receiving and acting upon constructive criticism.

A cornerstone of growth-oriented feedback is the collaborative establishment of development goals. Once areas for improvement have been identified and discussed, the natural next step is to work together to set specific, measurable, achievable, relevant, and time-bound (SMART) goals. This process ensures that the employee takes ownership of their development plan and feels invested in its success. For example, if the feedback was on improving public speaking skills, a collaboratively set goal might be: "To deliver a 10-minute presentation to the department on Project X, incorporating two new audience engagement techniques, by the end of the next quarter, with a self-assessment score of at least 8 out of 10 on clarity and impact." This SMART goal provides a clear target, a framework for progress, and a quantifiable measure of success. It transforms abstract feedback into tangible developmental milestones, empowering the individual to actively pursue their growth.

The process of receiving feedback is as critical as the process of giving it. Organizations that champion growth-oriented feedback also cultivate environments where employees feel empowered to seek it out. This can be encouraged through regular check-ins, where employees are prompted to ask for feedback on specific aspects of their performance or projects. It also involves training employees on how to interpret and respond to feedback effectively, teaching them to view it as a valuable resource for their career advancement. When individuals proactively seek feedback, they signal a genuine commitment to learning and improvement, which in turn fosters a more dynamic and adaptive organizational culture. This reciprocal relationship between providing and receiving feedback creates a virtuous cycle of development.

Positive reinforcement is an integral component of growth-oriented feedback. Recognizing and celebrating progress and achievements, no matter how small, is vital for reinforcing desired behaviors and maintaining motivation. When an employee successfully implements feedback, demonstrates a new skill, or achieves a developmental goal, acknowledging this success publicly or privately can have a profound impact. This could be a verbal commendation in a team meeting, a written thank-you note highlighting their effort, or even a small reward or recognition. For instance, if an employee has been working on improving their project management skills and successfully navigates a complex project milestone, acknowledging their meticulous planning and execution reinforces those valuable behaviors. This not only boosts the individual's confidence but also serves as a positive example for other team members, demonstrating that their commitment to growth is seen and valued.

The effectiveness of growth-oriented feedback is amplified when it is integrated into regular performance conversations and development discussions. Rather than being a singular event, feedback should be an ongoing dialogue. This can be facilitated through structured one-on-one meetings, performance reviews that emphasize development, and informal check-ins. By consistently providing and soliciting feedback, leaders help to normalize the process, making it a natural part of the work experience. This continuous feedback loop ensures that individuals are always aware of their progress, can address challenges proactively, and remain aligned with organizational expectations and goals. It moves away from the idea of feedback as a formal, often stressful, event, and towards a continuous, supportive process that fuels ongoing development.

Consider the impact of feedback on an employee who is new to a role. Initially, they might be hesitant to take initiative, unsure of the unspoken norms and expectations. Providing consistent, growth-oriented feedback during their onboarding period can significantly accelerate their learning curve and build their confidence. For example, a manager might observe a new hire's approach to a customer interaction. Instead of waiting for a formal review, they could offer immediate, specific feedback after the call: "I noticed you actively listened to the customer's concerns and empathized with their situation – that's excellent. To further enhance your ability to resolve issues, consider also asking clarifying questions to pinpoint the exact cause of the problem. Perhaps something like, 'To ensure I fully understand, could you tell me more about X?' This will help you gather all the necessary details for a comprehensive solution." This timely and targeted feedback allows the new employee to adjust their approach in real-time, fostering rapid skill development and preventing the entrenchment of ineffective habits.

The language used in delivering feedback plays a pivotal role in its reception. Employing "I" statements can depersonalize the feedback and focus it on observable behaviors and their impact. For example, instead of saying, "Your report was poorly organized," a more effective approach would be, "I found it challenging to follow the logical progression of information in the report. Perhaps organizing it by theme rather than chronology might improve its clarity for the reader." Similarly, focusing on future actions rather than past mistakes can be more constructive. Phrases like "Moving forward, let's focus on..." or "An area for us to develop together is..." shift the emphasis from what went wrong to what can be done better. This framing encourages a forward-looking perspective, essential for growth and improvement.

Building a culture where feedback is a shared responsibility is also critical. This means encouraging peer-to-peer feedback, where team members can offer constructive insights to one another. When feedback is a two-way street, it fosters a sense of shared accountability for development. This can be facilitated through team-building activities that incorporate feedback mechanisms or by establishing guidelines for how to give and receive peer feedback respectfully and effectively. For instance, a project team could implement a "lessons learned" session after each project phase, where individuals share what went well, what could have been improved, and what they learned from their colleagues. This collaborative approach to feedback not only enhances individual development but also strengthens team cohesion and collective problem-solving capabilities.

The impact of growth-oriented feedback extends beyond individual performance to influence the overall organizational climate. When employees feel that their development is a priority, they are more likely to feel valued, engaged, and committed to the organization. This, in turn, can lead to reduced turnover, increased innovation, and a more positive and productive work environment. A culture that embraces constructive criticism as a tool for progress, rather than a sign of failure, becomes a breeding ground for talent. It signals that the organization is invested in its people, empowering them to reach their full potential. This investment in human capital is not just a matter of good practice; it is a strategic imperative for long-term organizational success and resilience.

Moreover, growth-oriented feedback serves as a powerful tool for identifying and nurturing emerging talent. By consistently providing developmental feedback, leaders can pinpoint individuals who demonstrate a strong capacity for learning, adaptability, and leadership. These individuals can then be provided with more challenging assignments, mentorship opportunities, and tailored development plans to accelerate their progression within the organization. This proactive approach to talent management ensures a robust pipeline of skilled and capable leaders for the future. For example, a manager might notice that a junior employee consistently seeks out new responsibilities and proactively identifies solutions to problems. By providing feedback that encourages them to lead small project initiatives and offering guidance on effective team leadership, the manager is nurturing a potential future leader.

The element of courage is also inherent in delivering effective growth-oriented feedback, particularly when addressing sensitive topics or performance gaps. It requires leaders to be direct yet empathetic, to provide constructive criticism without causing undue distress, and to maintain a focus on development. This often involves difficult conversations, but approaching them with preparation, clear objectives, and a genuine desire to support the individual's growth can make all the difference. Leaders must also be prepared to receive feedback themselves, demonstrating humility and a commitment to their own continuous development. This creates a model of openness and learning that permeates the entire organization, fostering a healthy and productive feedback culture.

Ultimately, growth-oriented feedback is not a one-size-fits-all solution. It must be adapted to the individual, the context, and the specific developmental need. Some individuals may thrive on direct, frequent feedback, while others may benefit from a more gradual approach. Understanding these individual differences and tailoring the feedback accordingly is a hallmark of effective leadership. This nuanced approach ensures that feedback is not only well-received but also maximally effective in driving development and reinforcing positive behaviors. By mastering the art of growth-oriented feedback, organizations can cultivate a workforce that is not only high-performing but also deeply engaged, continuously learning, and resilient in the face of evolving challenges. This commitment to empowering employees through constructive dialogue and positive reinforcement is a critical pillar in building a truly supportive and flourishing workplace.

Chapter 10
Data-Driven Path to Wellness

To effectively gauge the impact and success of our mental health and True Leadership initiatives, establishing robust Key Performance Indicators (KPIs) is paramount. These metrics serve as the compass, guiding our efforts and illuminating the path toward a healthier, more engaged, and productive workforce. Without clearly defined KPIs, we risk operating in a vacuum, making it impossible to ascertain whether our investments in well-being are yielding the desired results or if adjustments are necessary. This section delves into the critical process of identifying and defining these essential measurement tools, differentiating between leading and lagging indicators, and ensuring our chosen KPIs are strategically aligned with overarching organizational objectives and genuine employee well-being.

When we embark on the journey of measuring the effectiveness of our mental health and leadership programs, it's crucial to understand the distinction between leading and lagging indicators. Leading indicators are predictive in nature; they provide us with an early warning system, signaling potential future outcomes. They offer insights into the progress and adoption of our initiatives, allowing for timely interventions and course corrections before significant issues arise. Conversely, lagging indicators, while vital for understanding the ultimate impact, measure outcomes that have already occurred. They tell us where we have been but offer less foresight into where we are heading. A balanced approach that incorporates both types of indicators provides a comprehensive and actionable view of program performance.

Consider, for instance, a leading indicator for employee engagement in mental health resources. This might be the percentage of employees who have accessed an Employee Assistance Program (EAP) or participated in a stress management workshop within a given quarter. A rise in these numbers suggests that employees are aware of and utilizing the available support, which is a positive sign for future well-being. A lagging indicator in this same context would be a decrease in reported instances of burnout or absenteeism due to stress-related illness over the subsequent year. While the increase in resource utilization is a good sign, the reduction in negative outcomes is the ultimate measure of success. Both are essential for a complete picture.

The selection of relevant KPIs must be a strategic exercise, directly linked to the specific goals of our mental health and leadership development strategies. These goals often revolve around fostering a supportive work environment, enhancing employee resilience, reducing stress-related issues, improving job satisfaction, and cultivating effective leadership behaviors. Therefore, our KPIs should be designed to reflect progress in these critical areas. This means moving beyond generic metrics and identifying those that are most sensitive to the interventions we are implementing.

For a mental health initiative aimed at reducing workplace stress, relevant leading indicators might include the completion rates of resilience-building training modules, the number of employees who have set personal well-being goals within our internal wellness platform, or the frequency of manager-led discussions on mental health and workload management. These metrics indicate the engagement with proactive stress-reduction strategies. Lagging indicators for this same initiative could be a reduction in the number of short-term disability claims related to mental health conditions, a decrease in employee turnover attributed to burnout, or an improvement in scores on employee surveys related to work-life balance and stress levels.

When we consider True Leadership initiatives, the KPIs will naturally shift to reflect leadership capabilities and their impact on the team. Leading indicators here might include the participation rates in leadership training programs focused on empathy, active listening, and psychological safety, as well as the proportion of leaders who have undergone 360-degree feedback and have action plans in place for development. Another leading indicator could be the frequency of one-on-one check-ins between managers and their team members that explicitly address well-being and professional development. Lagging indicators would then encompass improvements in team performance metrics, a reduction in team-related grievances, higher scores on employee engagement surveys related to leadership effectiveness and support, and a demonstrated increase in employee retention within teams led by those who have completed leadership development programs.

The process of defining KPIs should be inclusive, involving input from various stakeholders, including HR, departmental leaders, and employee representatives. This ensures that the chosen metrics are not only relevant but also perceived as fair and meaningful. It's also crucial to ensure that our KPIs are SMART: Specific, Measurable, Achievable, Relevant, and Time-bound. A KPI that is vague or impossible to quantify will offer little practical value. For example, simply stating "improve employee happiness" is not a SMART KPI. A more effective KPI would be: "Increase the average score on the 'Manager Support' question within the annual employee engagement survey by 10% within the next fiscal year."

Moreover, it's important to establish baseline data for our chosen KPIs before implementing new initiatives. This baseline provides a starting point against which we can measure progress. Without it, it's difficult to determine if observed changes are due to our interventions or simply part of normal fluctuations. For example, if we aim to reduce absenteeism due to stress, we need to know the current average absenteeism rate before we can measure the impact of our new wellness programs.

The selection of KPIs should also consider the qualitative data that can enrich our quantitative findings. While numbers tell a part of the story, the 'why' behind those numbers is often revealed through qualitative insights. This can include feedback from focus groups, open-ended responses in employee surveys, anecdotal evidence shared by managers, or case studies illustrating the impact of our programs on individuals. For instance, a leading indicator might show an increase in the utilization of a mental health app, but qualitative feedback could reveal that employees find the app particularly helpful for managing anxiety before public speaking engagements, providing a deeper understanding of its value.

As we move forward with implementing our mental health and True Leadership strategies, it is essential to review and refine our KPIs regularly. The organizational landscape is dynamic, and what was relevant yesterday may not be relevant tomorrow. We must remain agile, adapting our measurement framework as our initiatives evolve and as we gain more insight into what truly drives employee well-being and effective leadership. This continuous evaluation ensures that our data-driven approach remains a powerful engine for positive change, consistently guiding us towards a workplace where every individual can thrive.

To further elaborate on the selection of appropriate KPIs, let's consider a scenario where an organization is launching a new program focused on fostering psychological safety within teams, a core tenet of True Leadership. A key leading indicator here would be the percentage of team members who report feeling comfortable speaking up with ideas, questions, concerns, or mistakes without fear of negative consequences, as measured through a pulse survey conducted quarterly. This metric directly assesses the perceived safety of the team environment. Another leading indicator could be the frequency of 'blameless post-mortems' or 'lessons learned' sessions conducted after project milestones or incidents, indicating a proactive approach to learning from experiences rather than assigning blame.

Complementing these, a lagging indicator for this psychological safety initiative might be a reduction in voluntary attrition rates, specifically within teams where the program has been actively implemented. If employees feel psychologically safe, they are more likely to feel valued, supported, and engaged, which in turn can lead to greater loyalty. Another lagging indicator could be an increase in innovation metrics, such as the number of new ideas submitted and prototyped by teams. When individuals feel safe to experiment and share nascent ideas, innovation is often a natural byproduct. We might also track the improvement in upward feedback scores regarding the manager's ability to create an inclusive environment where all voices are heard and respected.

When selecting KPIs for mental health initiatives, it's crucial to ensure they are sensitive to the nuances of mental well-being. For example, beyond general absenteeism, we could track presenteeism – the phenomenon of employees coming to work while unwell, leading to reduced productivity. While difficult to measure directly, proxy indicators like a decrease in project completion times or a rise in errors for specific tasks could, when combined with other data, suggest an increase in presenteeism. A more direct leading indicator might involve tracking the uptake of flexible work arrangements that can support employees managing mental health challenges, such as adjusted hours or remote work options.

Furthermore, it's imperative to consider the intersectionality of mental health and leadership effectiveness. A leader who fosters strong psychological safety is likely to have teams that are more resilient and better equipped to manage stress. Therefore, KPIs for one initiative can often serve as indicators for the other. For example, if a leadership development program successfully enhances managers' skills in empathetic communication, this could positively impact team members' reported stress levels and their engagement with mental health resources.

To ensure a comprehensive and data-driven approach, it's beneficial to create a KPI dashboard that consolidates key metrics across different categories of our initiatives. This dashboard should be accessible to relevant stakeholders and updated regularly. Visual representations, such as trend lines and comparison charts, can make the data more digestible and actionable. For instance, a dashboard might show the trend of EAP utilization alongside the trend of team engagement scores and the trend of leadership feedback on psychological safety, allowing for a holistic view of how these elements are interconnected.

It is also important to acknowledge that not all KPIs can be easily quantified. For instance, measuring a culture shift towards greater openness about mental health can be challenging. In such cases, qualitative data becomes even more critical. We can use survey questions that ask employees about their comfort level in discussing mental health at work or track the number of internal communication campaigns or events focused on destigmatizing mental health challenges. The success of these efforts might be indirectly reflected in improved scores on questions related to organizational support and belonging.

When setting targets for our KPIs, it's vital to be realistic yet ambitious. Targets should be set by industry benchmarks, our own historical data, and the specific context of our organization. It's often more effective to set incremental improvement goals rather than aiming for drastic changes overnight. For example, a target to increase leadership empathy scores by 5% in the first year, followed by another 5% in the second year, might be more achievable and sustainable than a target of a 20% increase in a single year.

The ongoing collection and analysis of data related to our KPIs should inform strategic decisions. If a particular mental health resource is being underutilized, we need to investigate why. Is it a lack of awareness, accessibility issues, or is the resource not meeting the needs of our employees? Similarly, if leadership development programs are not translating into improved team performance or well-being metrics, we must examine the content, delivery, or follow-up support for these programs. This iterative process of measuring, analyzing, and adapting is what makes a data-driven approach truly effective.

Ultimately, the definition and diligent tracking of KPIs are not merely an administrative task; they are fundamental to demonstrating the value of our investments in mental health and True Leadership. They provide the evidence needed to sustain these crucial programs, to advocate for their expansion, and to ensure they are continuously optimized to create the most positive and lasting impact on our employees and the organization as a whole. By rigorously applying a data-driven methodology to measure success, we solidify our commitment to fostering a workplace that is not only productive and innovative but also deeply supportive and conducive to the holistic well-being of every individual. This commitment to measurable progress transforms our aspirations for a healthier workplace from mere intentions into tangible, impactful realities.

To effectively gauge the health of our workplace culture and the efficacy of our leadership interventions in real-time, it's imperative to focus on a suite of specific leading indicators. These metrics act as an early warning system, providing immediate feedback on whether our strategies are gaining traction and if adjustments are needed *before* negative outcomes become entrenched. Unlike lagging indicators, which show us the results of past actions, leading indicators offer a glimpse into future performance and the ongoing momentum of our well-being and leadership initiatives. By monitoring these forward-looking signals, we empower ourselves to be proactive rather than reactive, steering our organizational culture toward sustained health and productivity.

One of the most potent leading indicators for assessing the foundational element of psychological safety is the regular deployment of pulse surveys. These are not comprehensive annual engagement surveys, but rather short, frequent questionnaires designed to capture the prevailing sentiment on specific aspects of the work environment. For psychological safety, pulse surveys might include questions such as: "On a scale of 1 to 5, how comfortable are you sharing a dissenting opinion with your team leader?" or "To what extent do you feel your contributions are valued, even when they differ from the norm?" Another critical question could be: "How confident are you that mistakes made at work will be treated as learning opportunities rather than grounds for blame?" The frequency of these surveys – perhaps monthly or quarterly – allows for the detection of subtle shifts in employee perception. A downward trend in scores for these questions, even if marginal, signals a potential erosion of psychological safety and warrants immediate investigation. This might involve deeper dives through focus groups or one-on-one conversations within affected teams to understand the root causes. For instance, a sudden dip in comfort levels sharing dissenting opinions might be linked to recent feedback from a specific leader that was perceived as dismissive, or a change in project management style that inadvertently stifles open dialogue. By identifying these trends early, leadership can intervene with targeted coaching for the involved managers or re-emphasize the importance of inclusive communication practices before morale significantly deteriorates or critical ideas are suppressed.

Closely intertwined with psychological safety is the perceived quality of one-on-one (1:1) meetings. These regular interactions between managers and their direct reports are a cornerstone of effective leadership and a powerful conduit for both support and development. As a leading indicator, the quality of these 1:1s can be gauged through a few key methods. Firstly, employees can be asked in pulse surveys about the effectiveness of their recent 1:1s. Questions might include: "Did your last 1:1 meeting feel like a valuable use of your time?" or "Did your manager actively listen to your concerns and provide constructive feedback during your last 1:1?" Another way to assess this is by tracking the presence and quality of specific agenda items during these meetings. This can be done through a self-assessment by managers, perhaps integrated into performance management systems, or through anonymized employee feedback. For example, a successful 1:1 might typically include discussion points on current workload, personal well-being, career development goals, and any obstacles the employee is facing. A leading indicator of strong leadership would be a high percentage of employees reporting that their 1:1s include these crucial elements, and that they feel heard and supported during these conversations. Conversely, if pulse surveys reveal that employees perceive their 1:1s as superficial, rushed, or solely focused on task completion without regard for personal context, this serves as a critical leading indicator that leadership effectiveness may be waning and that employees might feel disconnected or unsupported. This could prompt timely coaching for managers on how to conduct more impactful and supportive 1:1s, focusing on active listening, empathy, and goal alignment.

Employee participation in wellness programs is another vital leading indicator that can provide real-time insights into the engagement with and perceived value of the well-being initiatives we offer. This goes beyond simply tracking enrollment numbers; it involves looking at active engagement. For instance, if we offer a series of stress-management workshops, the attendance rates and, crucially, the completion rates of any follow-up exercises are key leading indicators. A high initial sign-up followed by a sharp drop-off in attendance or completion might suggest that the program content is not resonating, the timing is inconvenient, or participants aren't seeing the immediate benefits. Conversely, consistent attendance and high completion rates for modules focused on resilience building or mindfulness indicate that employees find these resources valuable and are actively incorporating them into their routines. Similarly, the uptake of digital wellness platforms, such as mental health apps or online coaching services, can be a strong leading indicator. Tracking the frequency of login, the completion of recommended activities, and the utilization of specific features (e.g., guided meditations, cognitive behavioral therapy exercises) can reveal which aspects of the digital offerings are most impactful. If we observe a steady increase in the use of an app's anxiety management tools, for example, this is a positive leading indicator that suggests employees are proactively seeking support for common workplace stressors. Conversely, a plateau or decline in engagement with certain program components might signal a need for program redesign, enhanced communication about benefits, or even the introduction of new offerings that better meet current needs. This data allows for agile adjustments to our wellness portfolio, ensuring that our investments remain relevant and effective in supporting employee well-being.

Feedback on workload manageability is a critical, albeit sometimes sensitive, leading indicator of potential burnout and disengagement. Employees who consistently feel overwhelmed by their workload are at higher risk of stress-related health issues, reduced productivity, and eventual attrition. To capture this in real-time, we can integrate specific questions into our pulse surveys. For example: "On a scale of 1 to 5, how manageable do you find your current workload?" or "Do you feel you have the necessary resources and time to complete your assigned tasks effectively?" Another approach is to ask about perceived work-life balance specifically in relation to workload: "How often do you find yourself working beyond your standard hours due to an unmanageable workload?" The regularity of these pulse checks allows us to identify teams or departments where workload perceptions are deteriorating. A consistent rise in employees reporting unmanageable workloads or a decrease in those who feel they have adequate time for their tasks is a clear leading indicator that interventions are needed. This might involve reviewing task distribution, re-evaluating project deadlines, or providing managers with training on effective delegation and resource allocation. It can also highlight the need for clearer communication about priorities and expectations, ensuring that employees understand what is truly critical and what can be deferred. By proactively addressing concerns about workload before they escalate into full-blown burnout, we can safeguard employee well-being and maintain productivity levels.

Beyond direct feedback on psychological safety, 1:1s, and workload, other leading indicators can provide a more nuanced view of workplace health. For example, tracking the frequency and nature of internal communication related to well-being and leadership development is important. Are leaders proactively sharing resources and updates on mental health initiatives? Are they openly discussing the importance of work-life balance? The presence of consistent, positive messaging from leadership about well-being and effective leadership practices serves as a leading indicator of a culture that prioritizes these values. Conversely, a lack of such communication, or inconsistent messaging, can signal a disconnect between stated organizational goals and the lived experience of employees.

Another valuable leading indicator can be derived from observing employee behavior and engagement in learning and development opportunities. Beyond formal wellness programs, this includes participation in optional workshops, engagement with e-learning modules on leadership or soft skills, and voluntary attendance at departmental knowledge-sharing sessions. A high level of voluntary engagement in continuous learning, particularly in areas related to personal development and leadership competencies, suggests that employees are motivated, invested in their growth, and feel supported by the organization in their pursuit of improvement. This proactive engagement is a strong leading indicator of a healthy and adaptive workforce. If we see declining participation in these voluntary learning opportunities, it might signal a lack of perceived value, insufficient time allocated for learning, or a general decline in employee morale and motivation.

The effectiveness of our feedback mechanisms themselves can also be a leading indicator. Are employees actively providing feedback through the channels we've established? Are they engaging with the pulse surveys, suggesting improvements in team meetings, or utilizing suggestion boxes? A vibrant feedback culture, where employees feel empowered and encouraged to share their thoughts and concerns, is a powerful leading indicator of an open, transparent, and responsive organization. Conversely, if feedback channels are largely silent, it might suggest a culture of reticence, a lack of trust, or a perception that feedback is not acted upon. This would prompt an investigation into why employees are not engaging and what changes might be needed to foster a more robust feedback loop.

Furthermore, observing the informal dynamics within teams can offer qualitative leading indicators. Are team members actively supporting each other? Do they celebrate successes collectively? Is there a sense of camaraderie and mutual respect? While these are harder to quantify, they can be observed by managers and through anecdotal feedback. A decline in these positive informal interactions, or an increase in reported interpersonal conflicts, can be early signals of underlying issues in team cohesion or leadership effectiveness. Managers who are attuned to these subtle shifts can then proactively address potential problems before they impact team performance or individual well-being.

The collection and analysis of these leading indicators require a robust infrastructure and a commitment to data-driven decision-making. Utilizing technology platforms that can administer pulse surveys, track engagement with digital wellness resources, and collate feedback from 1:1 meetings is crucial. However, technology alone is insufficient. We must cultivate a culture where data is not just collected but actively interpreted and acted upon. This involves training managers to understand their team-level data, providing them with tools and support to respond to trends, and ensuring that senior leadership is also reviewing these indicators to inform broader organizational strategies.

For instance, if a pulse survey reveals a widespread concern about workload manageability in a particular department, the data should trigger a conversation between the departmental head and the managers involved. This conversation should not be about assigning blame but about collaborative problem-solving. What are the specific project pressures? Are there process inefficiencies? Can resources be reallocated? By using the leading indicator data as a catalyst for constructive dialogue and action, we demonstrate that feedback is valued and that the organization is committed to creating a sustainable work environment.

Similarly, if data shows a decline in employee comfort sharing dissenting opinions, this should prompt an examination of recent leadership behaviors or communication patterns within affected teams. Perhaps a recent strategic decision was communicated without sufficient opportunity for input, or a particular manager's feedback style has become perceived as critical rather than constructive. Identifying the specific cause, often through follow-up qualitative feedback, allows for targeted interventions, such as leadership coaching focused on active listening and empathetic communication, or an organizational-wide reinforcement of the importance of diverse perspectives.

The key to leveraging leading indicators effectively lies in their real-time nature and the ability to connect them to actionable insights. A high participation rate in a resilience workshop is a positive sign, but if the subsequent pulse survey shows no improvement in employees' reported ability to manage stress, then we need to investigate why. Is the workshop content not translating into practical application? Are employees facing systemic stressors that the workshop alone cannot overcome? These questions, prompted by the interplay of different leading indicators, drive continuous improvement.

Ultimately, by diligently monitoring and responding to these leading indicators – from the perceived quality of one-on-one meetings and workload manageability to employee participation in wellness programs and the comfort level in expressing differing opinions – we create a dynamic system for fostering a healthier and more effective workplace. This proactive approach ensures that our well-being and leadership initiatives are not static programs but living, breathing strategies that adapt to the evolving needs of our employees and the organization, preventing issues before they manifest and continuously reinforcing a culture of support, engagement, and high performance.

While leading indicators offer a crucial forward-looking perspective, enabling us to steer our organizational well-being and leadership initiatives proactively, their true value is often understood and validated through the lens of lagging indicators. These metrics, by their very nature, represent the historical outcomes of our past actions, providing a definitive measure of the success or failure of our implemented strategies over time. They are the final report card, reflecting the cumulative impact of our leadership approach and our commitment to employee well-being on the fundamental health and performance of the organization. Unlike the real-time signals provided by leading indicators, lagging indicators tell us where we have been and, by extension, the effectiveness of the path we have taken. They are essential for a comprehensive understanding of impact, allowing us to connect current organizational realities to the strategic decisions and interventions made months or even years prior.

Chapter 11
The Success Metrics

One of the most significant lagging indicators of an organization's commitment to employee well-being and effective leadership is the **employee turnover rate**. A consistently low turnover rate is a powerful testament to a healthy work environment where employees feel valued, supported, and engaged. Conversely, high turnover, particularly among high-performing individuals, signals deep-seated issues within the organizational culture, leadership effectiveness, or the perceived fairness and sustainability of the work environment. When employees choose to leave in significant numbers, it often points to a failure in leadership to foster psychological safety, provide adequate growth opportunities, manage workloads effectively, or maintain a healthy work-life balance. Analyzing turnover data not only by overall rates but also by department, tenure, and performance level can provide granular insights. For instance, if a particular department consistently experiences higher turnover than others, it strongly suggests that the leadership within that department may be falling short in implementing supportive practices. Similarly, if high-potential employees are leaving the organization, it indicates a critical gap in leadership's ability to retain top talent, perhaps due to a lack of challenging opportunities, insufficient recognition, or a perceived absence of genuine care for their development and well-being. Tracking voluntary versus involuntary turnover also offers different perspectives; a high rate of voluntary turnover directly reflects employee dissatisfaction, while involuntary turnover might, in some cases, be an indicator of a more rigorous performance management system, though it should still be scrutinized for fairness and consistency. The cost associated with high turnover – including recruitment expenses, training new hires, lost productivity during the onboarding period, and the potential impact on team morale – can be substantial, making it a critical financial metric that directly links to the efficacy of leadership and well-being initiatives.

Another vital lagging indicator is the **rate of absenteeism and its insidious counterpart, presenteeism**. Absenteeism, defined as the rate at which employees are absent from work, can be a direct consequence of poor mental and physical health, often exacerbated by stressful work environments and ineffective leadership. Chronically high absenteeism can disrupt team productivity, increase the workload for remaining employees, and signal underlying issues of burnout, disengagement, or chronic stress. While occasional absences are normal and expected, a sustained upward trend in absenteeism, particularly unscheduled absences, warrants serious investigation. It might indicate that employees are not being provided with adequate support for their well-being, that their workloads are unsustainable, or that the work environment itself is detrimental to their health.

Presenteeism, on the other hand, is the phenomenon of employees coming to work sick or otherwise impaired, leading to reduced productivity, increased errors, and the potential to spread illness. This is a particularly damaging lagging indicator because it is often hidden. An employee who feels pressured to be at work despite illness, or who cannot afford to take a sick day, is a clear sign of a culture that does not genuinely prioritize employee health. This behavior often stems from a fear of falling behind, a lack of adequate sick leave policies, or a leadership style that implicitly or explicitly discourages taking time off for health reasons. High presenteeism not only reduces individual output but also poses a risk to the health of the wider workforce. It's a lagging indicator that suggests a disconnect between stated organizational values regarding health and the practical realities experienced by employees. The ultimate impact of both absenteeism and presenteeism is a significant drain on organizational productivity and financial performance, directly reflecting the long-term consequences of leadership's approach to employee well-being.

Burnout itself, as a pervasive and debilitating condition, serves as a critical lagging indicator of an unhealthy work environment and suboptimal leadership practices. While leading indicators might capture early signs of stress and overload, burnout represents the chronic, sustained state of emotional, physical, and mental exhaustion resulting from prolonged exposure to excessive demands and insufficient resources or support. Organizations experiencing high rates of burnout often see a cascade of negative consequences, including decreased employee engagement, higher turnover, increased errors, and a decline in overall productivity. Identifying burnout as a lagging indicator requires a multi-faceted approach. This includes analyzing data from employee engagement surveys that specifically probe for symptoms of burnout, such as feelings of exhaustion, cynicism, and a reduced sense of personal accomplishment. It also involves observing patterns in absenteeism and presenteeism, as these are often precursors to or consequences of burnout. Furthermore, qualitative data from exit interviews and performance reviews can provide anecdotal evidence of burnout among departing or struggling employees. A leadership team that is vigilant about burnout as a lagging indicator will actively look for these signs and understand that the underlying causes are often systemic, related to excessive workloads, lack of control, insufficient reward or recognition, breakdown of community, absence of fairness, and conflicting values. Addressing burnout effectively requires not just individual coping strategies but a fundamental re-evaluation of organizational policies, work design, and leadership behaviors that contribute to its prevalence. The reduction of burnout, therefore, becomes a key measure of success for leadership and well-being initiatives.

Overall employee engagement scores, typically measured through comprehensive annual or bi-annual surveys, represent a robust lagging indicator of the collective sentiment and commitment of the workforce. While pulse surveys offer real-time snapshots, engagement surveys provide a more holistic and deeply analyzed view of how employees perceive their work, their leaders, and the organization as a whole. High employee engagement scores are a strong indicator that leadership has successfully fostered a positive work environment, instilled a sense of purpose, provided opportunities for growth and development, and effectively communicated organizational goals and values. Conversely, low engagement scores are a red flag, suggesting widespread dissatisfaction, a lack of connection to the organization's mission, or a failure in leadership to create a supportive and motivating workplace. When analyzing engagement data, it's crucial to look beyond the overall score and delve into the specific drivers of engagement. Questions related to manager effectiveness, recognition and rewards, opportunities for career advancement, and the perceived impact of their work are particularly relevant. A decline in scores in these areas, even if the overall engagement score remains stable, can be an early warning sign that leadership's effectiveness in fostering these critical aspects of the employee experience is waning. The connection between employee engagement and organizational performance is well-documented. Engaged employees are typically more productive, innovative, and committed to customer satisfaction, directly contributing to financial success. Therefore, sustained improvements in employee engagement scores serve as a powerful lagging indicator of the long-term positive impact of true leadership and comprehensive well-being strategies.

The tangible impact of effective leadership and robust well-being programs can also be measured through key **financial and operational performance indicators**. While these might not directly measure "well-being" in a psychological sense, they are the ultimate outcomes that demonstrate the business case for investing in people. Metrics such as **productivity per employee**, **innovation output** (e.g., number of new ideas implemented, patents filed), **customer satisfaction scores**, and ultimately, **profitability and revenue growth** can all be influenced by the state of employee well-being and the quality of leadership. For instance, when employees are healthy, engaged, and feel supported by their leaders, they are more likely to be focused, creative, and go the extra mile for customers, leading to improved service and higher sales. Conversely, environments plagued by high stress, burnout, and poor leadership can result in reduced output, increased errors, customer complaints, and ultimately, a negative impact on the bottom line.

To effectively utilize these financial and operational indicators as lagging measures, it's essential to establish clear baselines and track trends over time, correlating them with the implementation of specific leadership and well-being initiatives. For example, if an organization implements a new program to enhance work-life balance and manager support and subsequently observes a sustained increase in productivity per employee and a decrease in customer complaints related to service quality, these can be interpreted as positive lagging outcomes. Similarly, if investments in mental health support are followed by a reduction in absenteeism and an increase in profitability, this provides strong evidence of the tangible benefits of such programs. It's important to acknowledge that these financial and operational metrics are influenced by a multitude of factors, including market conditions, economic cycles, and competitive pressures. Therefore, a robust analysis requires careful consideration of these external variables and the use of statistical methods to isolate the impact of internal initiatives. However, by consistently monitoring these key performance indicators alongside more direct measures of well-being, organizations can build a compelling case for the long-term value and return on investment of their commitment to fostering a healthy, supportive, and effectively led workplace. These lagging indicators provide concrete proof that true leadership, grounded in employee well-being, is not merely a cost center but a critical driver of sustainable business success. They are the final, irrefutable testament to the positive transformation that intentional, people-centric leadership can bring about.

To truly understand the impact of your leadership and well-being initiatives, moving beyond the lagging indicators of outcomes like turnover and engagement scores to actively soliciting current employee sentiment is paramount. This is where the implementation of robust employee feedback mechanisms becomes not just beneficial, but essential. These mechanisms act as the organizational nervous system, constantly sensing the internal climate and providing real-time data that allows for agile adjustments and proactive leadership. They are the bridges that connect strategic intent with lived employee experience, ensuring that efforts to foster well-being and effective leadership are hitting the mark, or, just as importantly, revealing where course correction is needed. This section will delve into two primaries, yet distinct, methods for gathering this crucial qualitative and quantitative data: employee surveys and focus groups. Each serves a unique purpose in building a comprehensive picture of your organizational health, providing the nuanced insights necessary to refine strategies and demonstrate a genuine commitment to listening.

Employee surveys are perhaps the most common and widely recognized tool for systematically collecting feedback from a large workforce. When designed and deployed thoughtfully, they offer a scalable and efficient way to gauge employee sentiment on a wide range of topics related to well-being and leadership effectiveness. The power of surveys lies in their ability to quantify perceptions, allowing for trend analysis and benchmarking over time. However, their effectiveness hinges entirely on the quality of their design and execution. A poorly constructed survey can yield misleading or irrelevant data, while a well-crafted one can unlock invaluable insights that drive meaningful change.

The cornerstone of an effective employee survey is the quality of its questions. Questions should be clear, concise, and unambiguous, avoiding jargon or overly technical language that might confuse respondents. They should focus on specific behaviors, perceptions, and experiences rather than abstract concepts. For instance, instead of asking "Do you feel supported by your manager?", a more effective question might be: "My manager regularly provides me with constructive feedback on my performance," or "My manager shows genuine interest in my professional development." This specificity allows employees to anchor their responses to tangible experiences.

When designing questions related to leadership effectiveness, it's crucial to cover various dimensions of leadership impact. This includes aspects like:

Communication: How effectively do leaders communicate organizational vision, goals, and changes? Are they transparent and open? Do they listen actively? Questions might explore whether employees feel informed about company strategy, whether their leaders communicate clearly, and if they feel comfortable approaching their leaders with concerns. For example, "My direct manager communicates important information about company goals and performance in a timely manner," or "I feel comfortable approaching my direct manager with questions or concerns."

Support and Recognition: How well do leaders support their team members, both professionally and personally? Do they acknowledge and appreciate contributions? Are they approachable and empathetic? Questions could assess whether employees feel their contributions are recognized, if their managers provide the necessary resources to succeed, and if their managers are approachable. For instance, "My manager provides me with the resources and support I need to do my job effectively," or "My contributions are recognized and appreciated by my manager."

Development and Growth: Do leaders foster an environment that encourages learning and professional development? Do they provide opportunities for skill enhancement and career progression? Surveys can prove whether employees feel they have opportunities to learn new skills, receive constructive feedback for development, and have clear pathways for career advancement within the organization. Questions like, "My manager supports my professional development goals," or "I receive regular and constructive feedback that helps me improve my performance."

Fairness and Inclusivity: Do leaders treat employees equitably? Do they foster an inclusive environment where everyone feels valued and respected? Questions here might touch upon perceptions of fairness in workload distribution, opportunities, and treatment, as well as feelings of belonging and psychological safety. For example, "I believe my manager treats all team members fairly," or "I feel a sense of belonging within my team."

Well-being Advocacy: Do leaders actively promote and support employee well-being? Do they model healthy work habits and encourage work-life balance? Questions could gauge whether employees feel their managers encourage them to take breaks, manage their workloads sustainably, and prioritize their well-being. Examples include, "My manager encourages me to maintain a healthy work-life balance," or "My manager actively supports my well-being."

The frequency of surveys is another critical consideration. While annual engagement surveys provide a comprehensive, albeit retrospective, view, more frequent pulse surveys offer a real-time barometer of employee sentiment. Pulse surveys, typically shorter and more focused, can be deployed quarterly, monthly, or even more frequently to track changes in specific areas, particularly in response to new initiatives or significant organizational events. The key is to strike a balance: too frequent, and you risk survey fatigue; too infrequent, and you miss the opportunity to respond to emerging issues promptly. A common strategy is to combine an in-depth annual engagement survey with more frequent, targeted pulse surveys that drill down into specific aspects of leadership and well-being.

When deploying surveys, clear communication about their purpose, how the data will be used, and the commitment to anonymity and confidentiality is paramount. Employees must trust that their feedback will be handled responsibly and that it will genuinely inform action. Transparency builds trust, which is essential for honest and open responses. It is also vital to communicate the results of the surveys back to employees, along with the concrete actions being taken based on the feedback. Failing to act on survey feedback, or failing to communicate the actions taken, is a surefire way to erode trust and devalue the feedback process itself. This "closing the loop" demonstrates that employee voices are heard and valued, reinforcing the organization's commitment to continuous improvement.

Focus groups, in contrast to surveys, offer a more in-depth, qualitative exploration of employee perceptions. While surveys provide the "what" and "how many," focus groups excel at uncovering the "why" and providing rich, nuanced context. They involve small, carefully selected groups of employees (typically 8-12 participants) who are facilitated by a trained moderator to discuss specific topics related to well-being and leadership. This interactive format allows for the exploration of a wider range of perspectives, the identification of underlying themes and concerns, and the opportunity for participants to elaborate on their experiences in their own words.

The success of a focus group hinges significantly on the skill of the facilitator. The moderator must be neutral, adept at guiding the discussion without leading participants, and capable of creating a safe and open environment where diverse opinions can be shared freely. They need to be skilled in probing for deeper insights, managing dominant personalities, and ensuring that all voices have an opportunity to be heard. The questions used in focus groups are typically open-ended and designed to encourage discussion and exploration rather than simple yes/no answers. Examples include: "Can you describe what a supportive leader looks like to you?" or

"What are the biggest challenges you face in maintaining your well-being at work, and how do your leaders currently address them?"

Focus groups are particularly valuable for exploring complex or sensitive issues that might be difficult to capture through a structured survey. They can provide rich insights into the lived experiences of employees, revealing unspoken norms, cultural nuances, and the "unwritten rules" that shape the workplace environment. For example, a survey might reveal a general dissatisfaction with work-life balance, but a focus group can uncover the specific reasons why: unrealistic deadlines, a culture of 'always on' communication, or managers who do not model healthy boundaries. These details are crucial for developing targeted and effective interventions.

When selecting participants for focus groups, diversity of representation is key. It's important to include employees from different departments, roles, tenure levels, and demographic backgrounds to capture a broad spectrum of experiences. However, care must be taken to ensure participants feel comfortable sharing openly. Sometimes, bringing together a group of peers from the same department or level can be more effective than a mixed group, depending on the sensitivity of the topic. Anonymity and confidentiality must be clearly communicated to participants before the session begins, reinforcing that their individual contributions will not be identifiable.

The process of conducting and analyzing focus group data requires careful attention. Sessions are typically recorded (with participant consent) and transcribed for thorough analysis. The analysis involves identifying recurring themes, patterns, and key insights across the discussions. This qualitative data can then be used to:

Inform the design of future surveys: Insights from focus groups can help refine survey questions, ensuring they are relevant and capture the nuances of employee experiences.

Deepen understanding of survey results: When survey data reveals unexpected trends, focus groups can be used to explore the underlying reasons.

Develop targeted interventions: Understanding the specific drivers of issues identified in feedback mechanisms allows for the creation of more effective and tailored well-being and leadership development programs.

Co-create solutions: By involving employees in dialogue about challenges and potential solutions, organizations can foster a sense of ownership and increase the likelihood of successful implementation.

Integrating feedback mechanisms like surveys and focus groups into a continuous improvement cycle is vital. It's not enough to collect data; the real value lies in how that data is acted upon. This involves:

1. **Data Collection:** Systematically gathering feedback through well-designed surveys and thoughtfully facilitated focus groups.
2. **Analysis and Synthesis:** Rigorously analyzing both quantitative and qualitative data to identify key themes, trends, and areas for improvement. This stage may involve cross-referencing feedback from different sources to build a holistic picture.

3. **Action Planning:** Developing concrete, measurable, achievable, relevant, and time-bound (SMART) action plans based on the insights gained. These plans should be specific to identified issues and clearly assign ownership and accountability.
4. **Communication and Transparency:** Sharing the findings (both positive and areas for improvement) and the planned actions with the entire organization. This reinforces the value of feedback and builds trust.
5. **Implementation:** Executing the action plans. This is where the rubber meets the road, and the commitment to improvement is demonstrated.
6. **Measurement and Review:** Tracking the impact of the implemented actions using ongoing feedback mechanisms and lagging indicators. This cyclical approach ensures that efforts are continuously refined and that the organization remains responsive to the evolving needs of its employees.

The combination of surveys and focus groups provides a powerful dual approach to understanding employee sentiment. Surveys offer breadth and quantitative rigor, allowing for broad sentiment measurement and trend tracking. Focus groups provide depth and qualitative richness, enabling a nuanced exploration of issues and the discovery of underlying causes. By employing both, organizations can build a comprehensive, data-informed strategy for fostering employee well-being and enhancing leadership effectiveness, ensuring that leadership development and well-being initiatives are not just well-intentioned but demonstrably impactful and responsive to the actual experiences of the people within the organization. This commitment to listening and acting on employee feedback is a fundamental pillar of both effective leadership and a thriving, healthy workplace culture. It signals an organization that values its people and is dedicated to creating an environment where everyone can perform at their best, fostering both individual well-being and collective success. The insights gleaned from these mechanisms are not merely data points; they are the voices of the workforce, guiding the journey towards a more supportive, engaging, and productive future.

To truly embed a culture of continuous improvement in workplace well-being and leadership effectiveness, it is imperative to move beyond simply collecting data to actively use it for strategic advancement. This involves a deliberate process of benchmarking, goal setting, and iterative refinement, ensuring that your initiatives not only meet immediate needs but also drive long-term, sustainable progress. Benchmarking serves as the crucial first step in this evolutionary process, providing a vital external and internal context for your organization's current state.

Benchmarking involves comparing your organization's performance metrics against those of similar organizations or against your own historical data. This is not about a simple tick-box exercise; it's about gaining a realistic perspective on where you stand. When considering employee well-being, you might benchmark metrics such as absenteeism rates, employee burnout scores (as measured by surveys), participation rates in well-being programs, or reported levels of stress and workload management. For leadership effectiveness, benchmarks could include scores on leadership 360-degree feedback, employee engagement scores related to leadership support, or qualitative feedback on communication and fairness from focus groups.

The sources for benchmarking data are varied and can include publicly available industry reports, surveys conducted by reputable HR or well-being consultancies, and even data from professional networks. It's essential to select benchmarks that are relevant to your industry, organizational size, and geographical location to ensure a meaningful comparison. For instance, comparing your employee stress levels to a tech startup in Silicon Valley might be less insightful than comparing them to established manufacturing firms in your region if that's your industry. Similarly, internal benchmarking, tracking your own performance over time, is equally critical. This allows you to see the trajectory of your efforts and understand the impact of changes you've implemented. A steady decline in burnout scores over three years, even if still higher than industry averages, demonstrates positive progress driven by your strategies.

Once you have a clear understanding of your current performance through benchmarking, the next crucial step is setting meaningful goals. These goals should be derived directly from the data insights and should align with your broader organizational objectives. The SMART framework (Specific, Measurable, Achievable, Relevant, and Time-bound) is invaluable here. For example, if your benchmarking reveals that employee stress levels are 20% higher than the industry average and your own surveys indicate a lack of workload management support from managers, a SMART goal might be: "To reduce employee-reported stress levels related to workload by 10% within the next 12 months, as measured by annual employee surveys, by implementing enhanced manager training on workload delegation and time management techniques."

Achieving these goals requires a structured approach to continuous improvement. This is an iterative cycle where data collection informs analysis, which leads to action, followed by re-evaluation. The process looks like this:

1. **Data Collection and Analysis:** As discussed previously, this involves systematically gathering feedback through surveys, pulse checks, and focus groups, as well as tracking operational metrics like absenteeism or turnover. Analyzing this data reveals specific areas of strength and weakness.
2. **Identify Opportunities for Improvement:** Based on the analysis and benchmarking, pinpoint the key drivers of any identified issues. For instance, if engagement scores are low, the data might point to a lack of recognition or poor communication from middle management.
3. **Develop Targeted Interventions:** Design specific programs, training, or policy changes to address these identified opportunities. These interventions should be evidence-based, drawing on best practices and insights from your data. If the data suggests a need for better leadership communication, an intervention could be a series of workshops for managers on effective feedback delivery and transparent communication.
4. **Set Clear Objectives for Interventions:** For each intervention, establish specific, measurable goals that contribute to overarching organizational goals.

For the leadership communication workshops, a goal might be to see a 15% increase in employee scores related to manager communication within six months of the training.

5. **Implement Interventions:** Roll out the programs and changes with clear communication to all stakeholders. Ensure that employees understand the purpose of the initiatives and how they are expected to contribute to improvements.
6. **Measure and Evaluate Impact:** After implementation, reassess your key metrics. Did the leadership communication workshops lead to improved employee perceptions of manager communication? Use the same feedback mechanisms that informed the initial goal setting to track progress. This data is crucial for understanding the effectiveness of your interventions.
7. **Refine and Iterate:** Based on the evaluation, refine your interventions or develop new ones. If the workshops were successful but still didn't fully address the communication gap, further training or different approaches might be needed. If an intervention had no discernible impact, it's important to understand why and pivot your strategy. This continuous loop of measurement, evaluation, and refinement is the heart of continuous improvement.

The importance of actively tracking progress against your established goals cannot be overstated. This involves establishing dashboards or regular reporting mechanisms that clearly display your key performance indicators (KPIs) related to well-being and leadership. These reports should not only show the current status but also the trend over time, highlighting whether you are moving closer to or further away from your targets. For example, a well-being dashboard might track:

Employee Absenteeism Rate: Showing a month-over-month and year-over-year percentage change.

Employee Satisfaction with Work-Life Balance: Tracked through annual or quarterly surveys, displaying the average score and its trend.

Participation in Wellness Programs: Percentage of employees actively engaged in health initiatives.

Manager Effectiveness Scores: Aggregated scores from employee surveys related to leadership behaviors.

Reported Burnout Levels: Derived from specific survey questions designed to gauge burnout symptoms.

Regularly reviewing these KPIs in leadership meetings ensures that well-being and leadership development remain strategic priorities. It allows for the timely identification of any drift from the desired trajectory and facilitates prompt adjustments to strategies and interventions. For instance, if absenteeism rates begin to climb again after a period of decline, the leadership team can proactively investigate the underlying causes and implement corrective measures, such as re-evaluating workloads or reinforcing supportive management practices.

Furthermore, this continuous improvement cycle fosters a culture of learning and adaptation within the organization. When employees see that their feedback is being used to drive tangible improvements, it reinforces the value of their input and encourages greater participation in future feedback mechanisms. It also empowers leaders at all levels to see themselves as active contributors to the organization's well-being and effectiveness, rather than merely passive recipients of directives. This sense of agency and shared responsibility is a powerful catalyst for positive change.

The success of this continuous improvement framework also hinges on robust communication throughout the process. It's vital to transparently communicate the findings from benchmarking and data analysis, the goals that have been set, and the actions being taken. When interventions are launched, clearly articulate the "why" behind them and the expected outcomes. Equally important is communicating the results of these interventions and any adjustments being made to the plan. This "closing the loop" with employees is critical for maintaining trust and demonstrating a genuine commitment to progress. Without this transparent dialogue, even the most well-intentioned initiatives can falter due to a lack of buy-in or understanding.

For example, if your organization identifies a need to improve psychological safety through leadership practices, a series of training sessions on active listening and creating safe spaces for dialogue might be implemented. The communication plan would include:

Pre-launch: Announcing the initiative, explaining the data that informed it (e.g., survey results showing employees feel hesitant to voice concerns), and outlining the expected benefits for individuals and the organization.

During implementation: Providing updates on training progress and sharing resources for continued learning.

Post-implementation: Sharing aggregated feedback on the training itself, reporting on any observed changes in team dynamics or employee feedback related to psychological safety, and outlining any next steps or ongoing support mechanisms.

This iterative approach ensures that your well-being and leadership development strategies are not static but are dynamic, responsive, and constantly evolving to meet the changing needs of your workforce and the broader organizational landscape. By embracing benchmarking, setting data-driven goals, and embedding a cycle of continuous improvement, you create a virtuous loop that drives sustained enhancements in employee well-being, leadership effectiveness, and ultimately, overall organizational health and success. This commitment transforms well-being and leadership from mere HR initiatives into core components of your organizational strategy, directly impacting performance, resilience, and a positive employee experience.

Chapter 12
The 30-60-90-Day Implantation Roadmap
Part I

The initial thirty days of the implementation roadmap are dedicated to a thorough assessment of the current organizational landscape and the crucial task of building broad awareness around the True Leadership framework. This foundational phase is about establishing a clear baseline and fostering a shared understanding of why this initiative is not just beneficial but essential for our collective growth and success. Without a deep dive into our current realities and a concerted effort to engage every member of the organization, any subsequent actions, however well-intentioned, risk being misdirected or lacking the necessary buy-in to take root and flourish.

Our first undertaking in this critical assessment period is the deployment of comprehensive baseline surveys. These are not your typical employee satisfaction questionnaires; rather, they are meticulously designed instruments aimed at capturing nuanced data on two pivotal areas: psychological safety and overall employee well-being. Psychological safety, as we've established, is the bedrock upon which trust, innovation, and genuine collaboration are built. It's the shared belief that one will not be punished or humiliated for speaking up with ideas, questions, concerns, or mistakes. Measuring this requires questions that probe feelings of inclusion, the ease with which individuals can voice dissenting opinions, their comfort level in admitting errors, and their perception of risk associated with taking interpersonal risks within the team. For example, survey items might include statements like, "I feel safe to express my true thoughts and feelings at work," "It is easy for me to ask questions that might seem basic," or "I am comfortable admitting when I've made a mistake without fear of reprisal." The responses to these items, often captured on a Likert scale, will provide us with a quantitative measure of our current psychological safety climate.

Equally vital is the assessment of employee well-being. This encompasses a broader spectrum of an individual's experience at work, including their mental, emotional, and physical health. We will investigate factors such as perceived stress levels, work-life balance, workload manageability, feelings of burnout, and the availability and effectiveness of support systems. Questions here might focus on the regularity of feeling overwhelmed by work, the ability to disconnect from work during non-working hours, the extent to which employees feel their workload is manageable, and their perception of how well the organization supports their overall health. For instance, a question might read, "I regularly feel exhausted by my work," or "I am able to maintain a healthy balance between my work and personal life." These data points will paint a holistic picture of the current state of our workforce's well-being, highlighting areas of strength and, more importantly, areas that require urgent attention. The insights gleaned from these surveys will serve as our primary data source, providing the objective evidence needed to guide our subsequent strategic decisions and interventions. It's crucial to communicate the purpose and confidentiality of these surveys clearly to encourage honest and candid responses. Employees need to understand that their feedback is valued and will be used constructively to foster a better work environment.

Concurrently with survey deployment, we will undertake a comprehensive review of existing organizational policies and practices. This involves a deep dive into documentation, from formal HR policies and employee handbooks to informal operational norms and established workflows. We need to identify how current policies either support or, perhaps unintentionally, hinder the development of a True Leadership culture and positive employee well-being. This review will examine areas such as performance management systems, recognition and reward programs, communication protocols, conflict resolution procedures, and any existing well-being or mental health support initiatives. For instance, do our performance review metrics inadvertently encourage a win-at-all-costs mentality that could compromise psychological safety? Are our policies on flexible work arrangements robust enough to support work-life balance, or are they merely a superficial offering? We will also look at the practical application of these policies – are they consistently and equitably enforced across all departments and levels? This granular examination will uncover potential systemic barriers that need to be addressed. Engaging with department heads and HR representatives will be key to understanding how policies are interpreted and implemented on the ground. This review is not about finding fault, but about identifying opportunities for alignment and improvement, ensuring that our structural frameworks are conducive to the principles of True Leadership.

Simultaneously, we will initiate a robust and multifaceted communication campaign. The objective here is to introduce the concept of True Leadership to every individual within the organization, from the executive suite to the front lines. This campaign must be clear, compelling, and consistent, articulating what True Leadership means in our context and why its adoption is a shared imperative. We will leverage various communication channels, including company-wide emails, intranet articles, town hall meetings, team huddles, and potentially short video segments featuring leadership endorsements. The initial communications will focus on defining True Leadership – emphasizing its core tenets such as empathy, integrity, accountability, courage, and a commitment to fostering a supportive and growth-oriented environment. We will explain the 'why' behind this initiative, linking it directly to our organizational mission, values, and strategic goals, as well as the tangible benefits for both individuals and the collective. For example, a town hall meeting might feature senior leaders sharing their personal commitment to embodying these principles and explaining how this initiative will empower employees and create a more positive and productive workplace. This early communication is about planting the seeds of understanding and generating initial interest and engagement. It's vital that this messaging resonates authentically and avoids corporate jargon that might alienate employees. We want to foster genuine enthusiasm, not just compliance. The campaign will also clearly articulate the purpose of the upcoming surveys and the subsequent steps in the implementation process, setting expectations and encouraging participation.

Building on the initial communication, the focus shifts to deepening awareness and ensuring that the principles of True Leadership are understood at a practical, day-to-day level. This involves disseminating initial findings from our policy review, highlighting areas where existing practices may need recalibration to align with our True Leadership ethos. For instance, if the policy review identified that annual performance reviews are the only formal mechanism for feedback, communications might then introduce the concept of more frequent, informal feedback as a key component of True Leadership, encouraging managers and teams to adopt these practices. This isn't about immediate policy but about introducing new ways of thinking and operating. We will also begin to introduce anecdotal examples – carefully anonymized, of course – that illustrate what True Leadership looks like in action within our organization. These examples can come from nominations or observations, showcasing behaviors that exemplify empathy, effective communication, or a commitment to employee growth. Sharing these positive examples serves as a powerful way to make the abstract concepts of True Leadership tangible and relatable, providing role models and demonstrating the desired behaviors.

A critical element of this awareness-building phase is actively soliciting preliminary feedback on the proposed framework itself. While we are conducting structured assessments, we also want to create channels for open dialogue and early input. This could take the form of 'ask me anything' sessions with

HR or dedicated leadership development teams, or simply an open invitation for employees to share initial thoughts and questions via a dedicated email address or feedback portal. This proactive engagement helps to co-create the initiative, ensuring it feels relevant and responsive to the needs and perspectives of our workforce. It also helps to identify any immediate concerns or potential misunderstandings that can be addressed proactively. For instance, if employees express concern that "True Leadership" might be interpreted as a new set of unattainable performance metrics, the communication can immediately clarify that it is about fostering a specific culture and set of behaviors, not just a performance target.

Furthermore, we will begin to identify and engage "champions" or early adopters of True Leadership principles from across different departments and levels. These individuals, who may already exhibit many of these traits or are enthusiastic about the initiative, can become internal advocates, helping to spread awareness and provide peer support. Their involvement can be as simple as participating in early focus groups, providing feedback on communication materials, or sharing their experiences with their teams. Their authentic endorsement can significantly amplify the message and build credibility for the initiative. This process is about planting the seeds of a cultural shift. It's about making everyone aware of the journey we are embarking on, the reasons why it's important, and the initial steps we are taking to lay a solid foundation. By the end of this first 30-day period, our goal is to have established a clear picture of our current state regarding psychological safety and well-being, identified policy areas for attention, and generated a foundational level of awareness and understanding of the True Leadership framework across the entire organization, setting the stage for more targeted interventions in the subsequent phases. This meticulous groundwork is what will enable the successful implementation of our broader strategy, ensuring that our efforts are informed, inclusive, and ultimately, impactful.

The second month of our implementation roadmap, spanning days 31 through 60, marks a pivotal transition from awareness and assessment to active skill development and initial practice. Having established a foundational understanding of True Leadership principles and identified key areas for improvement in the first 30 days, we now move into a phase of equipping our leaders and teams with the concrete tools and behaviors necessary to embody these principles. This is where the abstract concepts begin to translate into tangible, everyday actions that will shape our organizational culture. The overarching goal of this period is to cultivate practical capabilities, encourage early adoption of new habits, and begin to embed True Leadership into the operational fabric of our organization.

A cornerstone of this phase is the rollout of targeted training programs specifically designed to build essential True Leadership competencies. These sessions are not generic leadership workshops; they are meticulously crafted to address the nuanced skills identified as critical for fostering psychological safety, enhancing employee well-being, and driving genuine engagement. We will prioritize training in empathetic communication, a skill that transcends mere politeness and delves into the ability to genuinely understand and respond to the emotions and perspectives of others. Training modules will explore techniques for active listening – not just hearing words, but truly processing the underlying meaning, intent, and emotional content. This includes practices like paraphrasing, asking clarifying questions, and demonstrating non-verbal cues that convey attentiveness and respect.

Another critical area of focus will be the development of skills in managing workloads and supporting employee well-being proactively. This involves equipping leaders with the ability to recognize early signs of stress or overload in their team members, engage in supportive conversations about workload, and collaboratively find solutions. Training will cover practical strategies for workload assessment, prioritization, and delegation, emphasizing how leaders can create an environment where employees feel empowered to discuss their capacity without fear of judgment. Furthermore, we will introduce techniques for delivering growth-oriented feedback – feedback that is constructive, specific, actionable, and delivered with the intention of fostering development rather than simply critiquing performance. This involves moving beyond the traditional annual review to embrace more frequent, informal feedback loops that are integrated into regular team interactions.

The delivery of these training programs will be multifaceted, employing a blend of learning methodologies to cater to diverse learning styles and ensure maximum retention and application. We anticipate using interactive workshops, facilitated discussions, case studies drawn from real-world organizational scenarios, and role-playing exercises to allow participants to practice new skills in a safe and supportive environment. For instance, in an empathetic communication session, participants might engage in simulated difficult conversations, practicing active listening and empathetic responses under the guidance of experienced facilitators. Similarly, a session on growth-oriented feedback might involve participants working in pairs to deliver feedback on hypothetical performance scenarios, receiving constructive input from their peers and the facilitator on their approach. The content will also be made accessible through online learning modules, allowing for flexible self-paced learning and reinforcement of key concepts.

Crucially, this phase emphasizes not just the acquisition of knowledge but the immediate application of these newly developed skills. Leaders will be actively encouraged to begin practicing these new habits in their daily interactions. This isn't about waiting for a formal policy change or a grand announcement; it's about integrating these behaviors into everyday conversations, team meetings, one-on-one check-ins, and problem-solving sessions. The expectation is that as soon as a leader participates in a training session on active listening, they should be consciously applying those techniques in their next team meeting or one-on-one conversation. This experiential learning is vital for internalizing the skills and building confidence in their application.

To support this transition from training to practice, we will establish robust support mechanisms. These will include a combination of individual coaching and peer learning initiatives. Individual coaching, provided by experienced internal facilitators or external consultants specializing in leadership development and mental health advocacy, will offer personalized guidance to leaders. Coaches will work with leaders to identify specific challenges they face in applying new skills, help them navigate complex interpersonal dynamics, and reinforce best practices. For example, a leader struggling with delivering difficult feedback might engage in one-on-one coaching sessions to role-play challenging conversations and receive tailored advice.

Peer learning groups, or "practice circles," will also be a significant component of this phase. These groups, comprising a small cohort of leaders from different departments, will meet regularly to share experiences, discuss challenges encountered during practice, and offer mutual support and accountability. These circles provide a valuable platform for leaders to learn from each other's successes and setbacks, fostering a sense of shared learning and collective growth. For instance, a practice circle might dedicate a session to discussing how members are implementing growth-oriented feedback, with each member sharing an example and receiving feedback from their peers. This collaborative approach helps to normalize the learning process and build a community of practice around True Leadership behaviors.

Beyond individual and team skill development, this 30-day period also involves the initiation of critical policy updates that directly support the True Leadership framework and employee well-being. Based on the insights gained during the assessment phase and the ongoing dialogue with employees and leadership, we will begin to formalize changes that reflect our commitment to psychological safety and holistic support. A key policy area to be addressed during this time will be related to mental health absences. This might involve revising existing sick leave policies to explicitly include mental health days, ensuring that employees feel safe and supported in taking time off for mental health reasons without undue scrutiny or stigma. This could also involve implementing clear guidelines for managers on how to handle conversations around mental health absences with sensitivity and support, reinforcing the organization's commitment to employee well-being.

Furthermore, we will commence the review and potential revision of performance management systems. The goal is to ensure that these systems are aligned with True Leadership principles, moving away from purely quantitative metrics that might incentivize unhealthy competition or discourage vulnerability, towards a more holistic evaluation that recognizes collaboration, learning, and contributions to team well-being. This might involve introducing new performance criteria that explicitly account for behaviors like active listening, supportive feedback, and fostering psychological safety. The process of updating these policies will involve a cross-functional team, including HR, legal, and representatives from various business units, to ensure that the changes are practical, legally sound, and effectively embedded within the organization.

The communication strategy during this phase will evolve to reflect the shift towards skill development and practice. We will provide clear and accessible information about the training programs being rolled out, their objectives, and how employees can participate. Success stories and examples of leaders and teams already demonstrating True Leadership behaviors will be actively shared through internal communication channels. This will serve to reinforce the importance of these skills, provide inspiration, and demonstrate the tangible impact of adopting these practices. We will also continue to provide avenues for feedback, encouraging leaders and employees to share their experiences with the training and the application of new skills, allowing for continuous refinement of our approach.

This second 30-day period is about building momentum and demonstrating tangible progress. By equipping our leaders with the skills, providing them with the support structures, and initiating the necessary policy adjustments, we are actively cultivating an environment where True Leadership can flourish. It's a phase that requires dedication from leadership to engage in learning and practice, and a commitment from the organization to provide the necessary resources and support. The focus on skill development and initial practice lays the groundwork for the deeper cultural integration that will characterize the subsequent phases of our implementation roadmap, transforming our understanding of leadership into lived experience. This phase is not merely about training; it is about cultivating a new mindset and embedding new behaviors that will ultimately redefine our organizational culture and drive sustainable success. The emphasis is on making these skills practical, actionable, and a natural part of our daily operations, moving beyond theoretical understanding to demonstrate competence and positive impact. The journey is about continuous learning and adaptation, ensuring that our True Leadership initiative remains relevant, effective, and deeply integrated into the fabric of our organization.

Phase 3 (Days 61-90): Integration and Reinforcement

Having diligently navigated the initial awareness and skill-building phases, the final thirty days of our 30-60-90-day implementation roadmap are dedicated to the crucial work of integration and reinforcement. This is where the seeds of True Leadership, shown in the preceding months, are nurtured to become deeply rooted, sustainable practices within our organizational culture. Our focus now shifts from introducing new concepts and practicing nascent skills to solidifying these behaviors, ensuring they become the norm, not the exception, and that the momentum generated is not only maintained but amplified. The ultimate aim is to transition True Leadership from a focused initiative into the very fabric of how we operate, how we lead, and how we interact on a daily basis, making it an indelible part of our organizational DNA.

A cornerstone of this integration phase is the systematic embedding of True Leadership principles into our established performance management systems. This is not merely about adding a few keywords; it's a deeper realignment to ensure that our evaluative processes actively recognize, reward, and encourage the behaviors that define True Leadership. We will meticulously review and, where necessary, revise performance review criteria to explicitly include competencies such as empathetic communication, proactive support for well-being, constructive feedback delivery, and the cultivation of psychological safety. For instance, an employee's or leader's ability to foster an environment where team members feel comfortable expressing concerns without fear of reprisal will be recognized as a significant contribution, not just a qualitative observation. Similarly, the consistent demonstration of active listening during team discussions and one-on-one interactions will be factored into performance assessments. This shift signals to every individual within the organization that these behaviors are valued, measurable, and integral to career progression and overall success. Performance improvement plans will also be recalibrated to incorporate development goals aligned with True Leadership competencies, providing leaders with clear pathways for growth in these critical areas.

Beyond formal performance reviews, we will also integrate these principles into our onboarding processes for all new hires, from entry-level staff to senior executives. From day one, new team members will be introduced to the organization's commitment to True Leadership. This will be communicated through orientation sessions, company policy documents, and early interactions with their managers and teams. Onboarding materials will highlight the importance of psychological safety, the expectation of empathetic engagement, and the value placed on well-being. For new leaders joining the organization, specialized onboarding modules will be developed that delve deeper into the practical application of True Leadership principles, including how to navigate team dynamics with an empathetic approach and how to leverage the support systems already in place. This ensures that our commitment to True Leadership is not a transient phase but a foundational element that shapes our workforce from its inception, creating a consistent understanding and expectation across the entire organization.

A critical element in reinforcing new behaviors is the active celebration and dissemination of early successes. We will establish platforms and communication channels to highlight instances where leaders and teams have effectively applied True Leadership principles, sharing these stories widely. This could involve internal newsletters, team meetings, all-hands calls, or dedicated intranet sections showcasing concrete examples of empathetic conversations that resolved conflict, proactive interventions that prevented burnout, or feedback sessions that genuinely fostered development and growth.

These success stories serve multiple purposes: they provide tangible proof of concept, demonstrating that True Leadership is not an abstract ideal but a practical and achievable reality; they offer valuable learning opportunities by illustrating effective strategies in action; and they serve as powerful motivators, inspiring others to adopt similar behaviors by showcasing the positive impact on individuals, teams, and the entire organization. Recognizing and rewarding these exemplary behaviors, whether through formal accolades or simple public acknowledgment, reinforces their importance and encourages their replication.

To further cement these practices, we will establish robust mechanisms for ongoing feedback and continuous improvement. This involves creating multiple avenues for individuals at all levels to provide input on the effectiveness of the True Leadership initiative and to share their experiences with its implementation. Regular pulse surveys specifically designed to gauge perceptions of psychological safety, leader support, and overall well-being will be deployed. Furthermore, we will encourage direct feedback through open-door policies, dedicated feedback channels (such as anonymous suggestion boxes or online forms), and regular "check-ins" that go beyond task-oriented discussions to explore how leaders are embodying True Leadership principles. This feedback loop is vital for identifying areas where further training or support may be needed, for refining existing strategies, and for ensuring that the initiative remains responsive to the evolving needs of our workforce. A continuous improvement committee, potentially comprising representatives from HR, leadership, and various employee groups, can be established to regularly review this feedback, analyze trends, and recommend adjustments to the

True Leadership program, ensuring its long-term relevance and effectiveness.

Peer learning and community building will also be a sustained focus during this integration phase. The practice circles and informal learning networks established in the previous stages will be encouraged to continue their work, perhaps evolving into more formal "champions" networks. These individuals, who have demonstrated a strong commitment to and proficiency in True Leadership behaviors, can serve as internal mentors and role models, providing ongoing support and guidance to their colleagues. We will facilitate opportunities for these champions to share best practices, lead informal training sessions, and champion the ongoing adoption of True Leadership principles within their respective departments or teams. Creating opportunities for leaders to connect and share their learning journeys, including both successes and challenges, fosters a sense of shared responsibility and collective ownership of the True Leadership culture. This could manifest as structured "lunch and learn" sessions, dedicated forums for sharing insights, or even cross-departmental mentorship programs focused on leadership development in these areas.

The communication strategy during this final 30-day period will be geared towards embedding the message of True Leadership as the established way of working. We will transition from communicating about the *introduction* of True Leadership to communicating about its *sustained practice* and *ongoing evolution*. This involves consistently reinforcing the core principles through all internal communication channels, ensuring that the language of empathy, support, and psychological safety becomes commonplace. Leaders will be encouraged to model this consistent communication, integrating True Leadership language into their daily interactions, team meetings, and strategic discussions. Success stories will be shared not as novelties, but as examples of our ongoing commitment. We will also proactively address any emerging challenges or resistance, providing resources and support to ensure that the integration is as smooth and effective as possible. Transparency about the ongoing efforts to refine and improve the True Leadership framework, based on feedback and evolving organizational needs, will be paramount.

Furthermore, we will assess the need for any policy or procedural adjustments that may have been identified as crucial during the earlier phases. This could include finalizing revisions to leave policies to explicitly support mental health or implementing more flexible work arrangements where appropriate to better support employee well-being. The goal is to ensure that our organizational infrastructure fully supports the desired leadership behaviors and creates an environment where True Leadership can thrive organically. This might involve ensuring that our resource allocation and reward structures are aligned with the values of psychological safety and support. For example, if a particular team consistently demonstrates high levels of collaboration and well-being, the company's recognition and reward systems should reflect this achievement.

The journey through this 90-day roadmap is designed to move our organization from a state of understanding and initial practice to one of ingrained cultural norms. Phase three is about making True Leadership not just a program or an initiative, but the fundamental operating system of our leadership and organizational culture. It's about ensuring that the commitment to employee well-being, empathetic engagement, and psychological safety is not only understood but actively lived out by every leader, in every interaction, every day. By integrating these principles into our performance systems, onboarding processes, communication strategies, and ongoing feedback mechanisms, we lay the groundwork for a truly sustainable and impactful transformation, where True Leadership becomes the enduring hallmark of our organization. This final push is about solidifying the change, making it resilient, and ensuring that it continues to evolve and strengthen over time, creating a workplace where every individual can thrive. The celebration of milestones achieved, coupled with a clear vision for the continued journey, empowers our people and reinforces the belief that this commitment is a long-term strategic imperative, not a fleeting trend. The focus is on making these learned behaviors second nature, ensuring they are applied with genuine intent and consistency, thereby fostering a workplace that is not only productive and high-performing but also profoundly human and supportive.

Chapter 13
The 30-60-90-Day Implantation Roadmap
Part II

Communicating the vision of True Leadership is not a mere announcement; it's a strategic imperative, the very bedrock upon which successful change is built. Without a clear, compelling, and consistently articulated vision, even the most meticulously crafted implementation roadmap will falter. Our goal here, as we progress through the initial stages of our 30-60-90-day plan and look towards deeper integration, is to ensure that every individual within the organization understands not just *what* True Leadership is, but *why* it matters, and *how* it will benefit them personally and collectively. This isn't about imposing a new set of rules; it's about fostering a shared understanding of a more effective, humane, and ultimately more successful way of working.

The initial days of our roadmap have focused on laying the groundwork – raising awareness and beginning the process of skill development. Now, as we move into the crucial phase of gaining widespread buy-in and effectively managing the inevitable shifts, our communication strategy must become more sophisticated and deliberate. We need to move beyond simply informing people to inspiring them, to making them active participants in this cultural evolution. This requires crafting messages that resonate deeply, identifying the right channels and voices to deliver those messages, and proactively addressing the concerns that naturally arise during any significant organizational change.

At the heart of effective communication is a clearly defined vision. This vision must be more than just a set of principles; it needs to be a compelling narrative that paints a picture of the desired future state. It should articulate the tangible benefits of True Leadership, not just for the organization's bottom line, but for the individuals within it. Think about the impact on employee engagement, the reduction of stress and burnout, the enhancement of collaboration, and the creation of an environment where innovation and creativity can truly flourish. These are powerful motivators that speak to the core human need for purpose, connection, and well-being in the workplace. When communicating this vision, we must be explicit about how True Leadership translates into everyday experiences. For instance, instead of saying "we will foster psychological safety," we might articulate it as "you will feel empowered to voice your opinions and concerns without fear of negative repercussions, knowing that your contributions are valued and respected."

To amplify the impact of this vision, we must identify and engage key stakeholders and influencers across the organization. These are not just senior leaders, but also middle managers, team leads, and even influential individual contributors who are respected by their peers. These individuals can act as powerful champions for the True Leadership initiative, translating the vision into their specific contexts and reinforcing its importance within their teams. Early engagement with these influencers is critical. In the first 30-60 days, we should have been identifying these individuals, perhaps through informal conversations or by observing those who naturally embody empathetic and supportive behaviors. Now, we need to equip them with the knowledge, resources, and support they need to champion the vision effectively. This could involve providing them with talking points, sharing success stories, and creating opportunities for them to discuss the initiative with their own networks.

Developing a comprehensive communication plan is paramount. This plan should outline the key messages, the target audiences, the communication channels, and the timing of our communications. It needs to be a multi-faceted approach, utilizing a variety of channels to ensure that the message reaches everyone, regardless of their role or location. Internal newsletters, town hall meetings, team briefings, dedicated intranet pages, and even personalized emails from leaders all have a role to play. The key is to ensure consistency across all channels. A message delivered in a company-wide email should be reinforced in a team meeting and echoed in one-on-one conversations.

Crucially, our communication plan must proactively address potential concerns and foster enthusiasm. Change, by its very nature, can be unsettling. Employees may worry about increased workloads, potential shifts in power dynamics, or a lack of genuine commitment from leadership. Our communication must acknowledge these potential anxieties and provide clear, reassuring answers. Transparency is vital here. We need to be open about the challenges we anticipate and the strategies we are implementing to mitigate them. For example, if there are concerns that implementing more supportive leadership practices might lead to a decrease in productivity, our communication should highlight how increased engagement and reduced stress can boost productivity in the long run. We should also be prepared to address any skepticism with concrete evidence and examples.

Demonstrating unwavering leadership commitment is perhaps the most critical element in gaining buy-in. Employees will look to their leaders for cues. If leaders do not visibly and consistently champion True Leadership principles, the initiative will quickly lose credibility. This means leaders must not only articulate the vision but also embody it in their own behaviors. Their communication should be characterized by empathy, active listening, and a genuine concern for the well-being of their teams. They need to be seen walking through the talk, not just talking the talk. This could involve leaders actively seeking feedback, admitting when they have made mistakes, and visibly prioritizing the well-being of their employees alongside business objectives. The 60-90-day period of our roadmap is precisely when this visible commitment becomes most impactful, as it reinforces the behavioral changes that are beginning to take root.

To build momentum and ensure that the vision is not just heard but felt, we need to cultivate enthusiasm actively. This can be achieved by celebrating early wins and highlighting positive examples. As leaders and teams begin to adopt True Leadership behaviors, these successes should be recognized and shared widely. This creates a virtuous cycle, where positive reinforcement encourages further adoption and inspires others. For instance, a department that successfully implements a new well-being initiative that leads to a measurable improvement in employee morale could be featured in an internal publication or recognized at a company-wide meeting. These stories serve as powerful proof points, demonstrating that True Leadership is not an abstract concept but a tangible and beneficial reality.

Furthermore, our communication strategy needs to be dynamic and adaptive. It's not a one-off event but an ongoing conversation. As we gather feedback and observe the impact of our initiatives, we must be prepared to refine our messaging and adjust our approach. This demonstrates a commitment to continuous improvement and ensures that our communication remains relevant and responsive to the evolving needs of the organization. Creating feedback channels, such as surveys or dedicated forums, allows employees to voice their perspectives and feel heard. This dialogue is essential for maintaining engagement and for identifying any areas where our communication might be falling short.

The language we use in our communications is also incredibly important. It should be inclusive, positive, and focused on empowerment. We want to foster a sense of collective ownership and shared responsibility for building a True Leadership culture. This means avoiding jargon or overly corporate language and instead opting for clear, accessible, and relatable communication. The aim is to make everyone feel that they are part of this journey and that their contributions are valued. When discussing the implementation of True Leadership, the focus should be on the positive outcomes and the opportunities for growth and development that it presents.

In the 30-60-day period, we focused on building awareness and initiating the practice of True Leadership behaviors. Now, as we transition to the 60-90-day integration phase, our communication efforts pivot towards embedding this vision as a core organizational value. This means ensuring that our internal communications consistently reinforce the principles of empathetic leadership, psychological safety, and proactive well-being support. It's about making these concepts part of the everyday vernacular, so that they are no longer perceived as a new initiative, but as the inherent way we operate. Leaders at all levels must be encouraged to weave these themes into their regular team discussions, strategic planning sessions, and one-on-one interactions. The goal is to move from announcing "we are implementing True Leadership" to demonstrating "this is how we lead."

The transition requires a conscious effort to shift the narrative from a change management process to a continuous cultural evolution. Success stories, which were perhaps highlighted as novelties in the earlier phases, now need to be presented as ongoing examples of our commitment. Sharing instances where empathetic conversations have resolved complex issues, where proactive support has prevented team burnout, or where constructive feedback has genuinely accelerated development serves as more than just proof of concept; it provides practical, relatable learning opportunities and reinforces the value of these behaviors through positive peer influence. This consistent reinforcement is key to ensuring that True Leadership is not a fleeting trend but a deeply ingrained aspect of the organizational culture.

To truly gain buy-in and manage this cultural shift effectively, transparency in our communication is paramount. This means openly sharing progress, acknowledging challenges, and providing clear pathways for ongoing feedback. As we implement True Leadership principles, we might encounter unforeseen obstacles or receive feedback that necessitates adjustments to our approach. Communicating these realities openly fosters trust and demonstrates a commitment to an adaptive, iterative process. This transparency extends to the very nature of the True Leadership framework itself. By openly discussing how the initiative is being refined based on feedback and evolving organizational needs, we empower employees to feel like active contributors to the shaping of their workplace environment. This proactive engagement builds a sense of shared ownership, making the adoption of True Leadership principles a collective endeavor rather than a top-down directive.

Moreover, communication must extend beyond mere articulation to active demonstration. Leaders must be seen as the primary exemplars of True Leadership. Their words need to be backed by consistent actions. This means prioritizing empathetic communication in all interactions, actively listening to concerns without interruption, and demonstrating genuine support for employee well-being. When leaders consistently model these behaviors, it creates a powerful ripple effect throughout the organization, inspiring others to follow suit. This visible commitment is the most effective tool for overcoming inertia and fostering genuine enthusiasm for the cultural shift. It signals that True Leadership is not an optional extra, but a fundamental expectation for all who hold leadership positions.

Building momentum for the implementation roadmap also relies on a communication strategy that highlights the broader organizational benefits. While individual well-being and team dynamics are crucial, it's equally important to articulate how True Leadership contributes to overarching business objectives. This could involve linking improved employee engagement to increased productivity, reduced absenteeism, and enhanced innovation. When employees understand that embracing True Leadership not only creates a better work environment but also contributes to the organization's success, their buy-in deepens. This strategic communication ensures that the initiative is viewed not as a 'soft' skill development program, but as a vital component of organizational strategy, driving both human and business outcomes.

The communication plan must also be designed to cater to different learning styles and preferences. While some individuals may absorb information through written materials or formal presentations, others might benefit more from interactive workshops, peer discussions, or personal coaching. Therefore, the communication strategy should incorporate a variety of methods to ensure that the message of True Leadership is accessible and impactful for everyone. This could include offering optional learning sessions, creating mentorship opportunities where experienced leaders can guide others, or developing easily digestible digital resources that employees can access at their own pace. By providing multiple avenues for engagement, we cater to a diverse workforce and maximize the reach and effectiveness of our communication efforts.

In essence, communicating the vision of True Leadership is an ongoing, dynamic process that requires strategic planning, consistent execution, and a genuine commitment to transparency and inclusivity. It's about crafting a compelling narrative, engaging key influencers, utilizing diverse communication channels, proactively addressing concerns, and consistently demonstrating leadership commitment. By investing in effective communication, we lay the essential groundwork for widespread buy-in, successfully manage the cultural shift, and build the momentum needed to embed True Leadership as the enduring hallmark of our organization, ensuring that our 30-60-90-day plan culminates in a truly sustainable and impactful transformation. The ultimate aim is to create a shared understanding and a collective aspiration for a workplace that is not only productive and high-performing but also deeply human, supportive, and ultimately, truly leading.

Embarking on the journey of integrating True Leadership principles across an entire organization is a significant undertaking, one that demands careful planning and execution to ensure lasting impact and widespread adoption. While the initial phases of our 30-60-90-day roadmap have focused on laying the foundational awareness and beginning the practice of these principles, the subsequent stages necessitate a strategic approach to broad implementation. To mitigate risks, gather invaluable insights, and tailor the rollout for maximum effectiveness, the judicious use of pilot programs is not merely beneficial; it is a critical component of a robust implementation strategy. This approach allows us to test the waters, refine our strategies based on real-world feedback, and build confidence and momentum before a full-scale deployment.

The concept of a pilot program is rooted in the principle of iterative development – a cyclical process of planning, executing, evaluating, and refining. In the context of True Leadership, this means selecting a representative subset of the organization to test the proposed initiatives, policies, and training modules. This smaller, controlled environment serves as a living laboratory, where we can observe firsthand how the principles translate into practice, identify unforeseen challenges, and gather crucial feedback from those directly experiencing the changes. The insights gleaned from a pilot program are invaluable, enabling us to make informed adjustments to our approach, thereby increasing the likelihood of success when we eventually scale the initiative across the entire organization. It's about moving from a theoretical understanding to a practical, evidence-based application.

Selecting the right participants for a pilot program is paramount to its success. Ideally, a pilot group should be representative of the broader organizational diversity in terms of departments, roles, seniority levels, and even geographical locations if applicable. This ensures that the feedback received is comprehensive and accounts for the varied experiences and perspectives that exist within the organization. For instance, a pilot involving a customer-facing team might reveal different challenges and opportunities compared to a pilot with a research and development department. Aiming for a mix of enthusiastic early adopters and those who might be more skeptical can also provide valuable insights into how to address potential resistance during a wider rollout. The size of the pilot group should be substantial enough to generate meaningful data but small enough to be effectively managed and supported. This might range from a single department to a cross-functional team comprised of individuals from various units.

Once the pilot participants have been identified, it is essential to clearly define the objectives and success criteria for the pilot program. What specific outcomes are we hoping to achieve? Are we looking to see an improvement in employee engagement scores, a reduction in reported stress levels, an increase in collaborative behaviors, or enhanced psychological safety? Establishing measurable Key Performance Indicators (KPIs) before the pilot begins provides a clear benchmark against which to evaluate its effectiveness. These criteria should be aligned with the overarching goals of the True Leadership initiative. For example, if a key objective is to foster more empathetic communication, a success criterion might be an increase in positive feedback regarding communication clarity and supportiveness in team interactions, as measured through post-pilot surveys.

The pilot phase should not be a static implementation; rather, it should be an active learning period. This involves systematically collecting feedback throughout the program's duration. Various methods can be employed for this purpose. Regular pulse surveys can gauge sentiment and identify emerging issues. Focus groups, conducted at key intervals, allow for more in-depth qualitative feedback, enabling participants to elaborate on their experiences, share specific examples, and offer suggestions for improvement. One-on-one interviews with pilot participants and their direct managers can provide further nuanced insights. Crucially, the feedback mechanism should be designed to be accessible, anonymous where appropriate, and to actively encourage constructive criticism. It's not just about what's working, but also what isn't and why.

Once the pilot program is underway, the data and feedback collected must be meticulously analyzed. This analysis should go beyond simply noting whether objectives were met. It requires a deeper dive into the qualitative data to understand the underlying reasons for observed behaviors and attitudes. Were there specific training modules that resonated more strongly? Were there any leadership behaviors that were particularly effective or counterproductive? Were there any organizational processes that hindered the adoption of True Leadership principles? This detailed analysis is the foundation for making informed decisions about refining the program before a broader rollout. It's about identifying the 'why' behind the 'what'.

The insights gained from the pilot program then inform an iterative refinement of the True Leadership initiatives. This might involve revising training materials to be more engaging or practical, adjusting communication strategies, modifying policies to better support the desired behaviors, or providing additional resources and support for leaders. For example, if the pilot revealed that managers struggled with having difficult conversations, the revised program might include more targeted training or role-playing exercises focused on these scenarios. If feedback indicated that the initial goals were too ambitious for the given timeframe, they might be adjusted for the wider rollout. This iterative process ensures that the program becomes increasingly robust and aligned with the organization's unique culture and needs.

With the refined program in hand, the next logical step is to plan for a phased or iterative rollout. A "big bang" approach, where the initiative is launched across the entire organization simultaneously, can be overwhelming and disruptive. A phased approach, on the other hand, allows for a more controlled and manageable transition. This can take various forms. A departmental rollout, where the program is implemented one department at a time, allows for focused attention and learning from each stage. Alternatively, a team-based rollout, starting with a few key teams and gradually expanding, can also be effective, particularly in larger, more complex organizations. This allows for a more granular approach to implementation and support.

When planning a phased rollout, it's crucial to consider the sequencing. Which departments or teams should be prioritized? Often, it makes sense to start with areas that have shown the most enthusiasm or readiness for change, or those where the impact of True Leadership would be most acutely felt. Conversely, starting with a pilot within a more challenging department might provide valuable lessons on overcoming resistance. The pace of the rollout is also critical. It should be deliberate enough to allow for proper training, support, and integration, but not so slow that it loses momentum.

Each phase of the rollout should include a mechanism for ongoing feedback and continuous improvement. The lessons learned from the initial pilot should inform the implementation in subsequent phases. This creates a virtuous cycle of learning and adaptation, ensuring that the program evolves as it is rolled out. Regular check-ins with teams and departments, post-implementation surveys, and ongoing performance monitoring are essential for identifying any new challenges or opportunities for enhancement. It’s about recognizing that the implementation of True Leadership is not a one-time event, but an ongoing commitment to development and adaptation.

Furthermore, the communication strategy for the rollout must be continually reinforced and adapted. As the program expands to new groups, consistent messaging is vital, but it should also be tailored to address the specific concerns and context of each new group. Early successes from previous phases should be communicated to build confidence and enthusiasm in upcoming groups. Transparency about the process – sharing what was learned from the pilot and how the program has been adapted – is key to fostering trust and encouraging engagement. This communication should highlight not just the 'what' but also the 'why' and the 'how' for each new group being brought into the fold.

The success of a phased rollout also depends heavily on the ongoing support provided to leaders and employees. This might include continued access to training resources, coaching for managers who are new to implementing True Leadership principles, and dedicated support channels for questions and concerns. As the program moves into different phases, the nature of the support might need to evolve. For example, in the initial phases, support might focus on understanding the concepts, while in later phases, it might shift towards refining practices and addressing more complex leadership challenges.

It is also important to acknowledge that not every pilot program or every phase of a rollout will go exactly as planned. There will inevitably be unexpected challenges and setbacks. The key is to approach these with a problem-solving mindset, leveraging the feedback mechanisms and iterative processes that have been established. The ability to adapt and learn from these challenges is a hallmark of True Leadership itself, and by modeling this approach during the implementation, the organization reinforces the very principles it seeks to instill. This resilience in the face of difficulty is what ultimately builds a sustainable culture.

The selection of pilot groups should also consider how well they can serve as internal champions for the broader rollout. Participants who have had a positive experience and can articulate the benefits of True Leadership in their own words can become powerful advocates. Identifying these individuals and empowering them to share their experiences can be a highly effective strategy for driving buy-in across the organization. This peer-to-peer influence can often be more persuasive than top-down communication alone.

In essence, the strategy of using pilot programs and iterative rollout allows for a measured and responsive approach to embedding True Leadership. It is a testament to a mature understanding of organizational change – recognizing that a one-size-fits-all approach is rarely effective. By investing the time and resources to test, refine, and gradually implement, organizations can significantly increase the chances of not only successful adoption but also of creating a deeply ingrained culture of True Leadership that drives sustainable positive impact for both individuals and the organization as a whole. This methodical approach ensures that the journey towards True Leadership is one of continuous learning, adaptation, and ultimately, profound and lasting transformation. The data gathered from these pilot phases provides the bedrock for the subsequent, more widespread implementation, ensuring that the strategies are not only aligned with the vision but also practical and resonant with the lived experiences of the people within the organization. This ensures that the transition is not just a change in practice, but a genuine evolution of organizational consciousness.

Chapter 14
Prioritizing Mental Health

The journey of fostering a culture of care within an organization, as we've discussed, hinges significantly on the behaviors and capacity of its leaders. While our focus has been on empowering leaders to support their teams, it's imperative to address a critical paradox: the very leaders who champion well-being are often at a heightened risk of experiencing burnout themselves. The relentless demands of leadership, coupled with the empathetic labor required to truly care for a team, can create a perfect storm for exhaustion. Therefore, recognizing and actively addressing leader burnout is not a secondary concern; it is an absolute leadership imperative. Without leaders who are personally resilient and sustainably practicing self-care, the efforts to cultivate a caring environment will inevitably falter, proving to be unsustainable and, at worst, performative.

To truly embed a culture of care, leaders must first and foremost embody it within themselves. This means acknowledging that their own well-being is not a personal indulgence but a professional necessity. When leaders neglect their own mental, emotional, and physical health, they not only diminish their effectiveness but also inadvertently signal to their teams that personal sacrifice is the ultimate measure of dedication. This message can perpetuate unhealthy work habits throughout the organization. Therefore, commitment to self-care must be viewed as a strategic component of leadership, essential for long-term organizational health and the ability to consistently provide the support and guidance that teams need.

The pressures faced by leaders can be immense and multifaceted. They are often the primary conduits for organizational directives, the first point of contact for employee concerns, and the ultimate decision-makers in high-stakes situations. This constant state of readiness and responsibility can lead to chronic stress, a persistent feeling of being overwhelmed, and a depletion of personal resources. Without proactive strategies to manage these demands, leaders can find themselves trapped in a cycle of exhaustion, leading to decreased cognitive function, emotional detachment, and a reduced capacity for empathy – precisely the qualities that define authentic, caring leadership.

One of the foundational elements of addressing leader burnout is the deliberate cultivation of personal stress management techniques. This is not about eliminating stress entirely, which is often an unrealistic goal in demanding leadership roles, but about developing a robust toolkit to navigate and mitigate its negative effects. Mindfulness and meditation, for instance, offer powerful pathways to regain a sense of calm and presence amidst chaos. Even short, consistent periods of focused breathing or a brief guided meditation can significantly reduce physiological stress responses, allowing leaders to approach challenges with greater clarity and composure. Incorporating these practices into daily routines, perhaps at the start of the day, before a challenging meeting, or during a brief break, can create crucial moments of respite and recalibration. The key is consistency; even five minutes daily can yield substantial benefits over time, acting as a personal anchor in turbulent professional waters.

Beyond mindfulness, engaging in regular physical activity is another vital, though often overlooked, component of stress management for leaders. Exercise is a potent antidote to the wear and tear of chronic stress, helping to reduce levels of cortisol, the body's primary stress hormone, and boost the production of endorphins, which have mood-lifting effects. This doesn't necessitate demanding, time-consuming workouts. A brisk walk during a lunch break, taking the stairs instead of the elevator, or even a short stretching routine can make a tangible difference. The physical act of moving the body can also serve as a mental release, providing a valuable distraction from pressing work concerns and allowing for a fresh perspective. Leaders who prioritize physical health are better equipped to handle the sustained demands of their roles, demonstrating resilience that can be both seen and felt by their teams.

Crucially, leaders must also become adept at setting clear and firm boundaries. In an era of constant connectivity, the lines between work and personal life can easily blur, leading to a pervasive sense of being "always on." This can be particularly challenging for leaders who feel a deep sense of responsibility for their teams' well-being. However, to be truly effective and sustainable, boundaries are non-negotiable. This involves defining specific times for work and times for rest and personal engagement and then adhering to these boundaries as rigorously as possible. It might mean designating certain hours when email and phone calls are not checked or establishing a clear ritual for transitioning from work mode to personal time at the end of the day. Communicating these boundaries to the team, not as a sign of disengagement, but as a commitment to sustainable performance, is also important. For example, a leader might inform their team that they will respond to non-urgent queries within 24 hours, setting a clear expectation that respects both their own time and the team's needs.

Seeking and accepting support is another critical, yet often challenging, aspect of leader self-care. Many leaders operate under the assumption that they must have all the answers and that seeking help is a sign of weakness. This is a dangerous misconception. In reality, recognizing when one needs assistance and actively seeking it is a profound demonstration of strength and self-awareness. This support can come in various forms. Mentorship, either from a more senior leader within the organization or from an external professional, can provide invaluable guidance and perspective. Peer support networks, where leaders can connect with others facing similar challenges, can offer a safe space to share experiences, brainstorm solutions, and validate their feelings. Executive coaching is also a powerful resource, providing a confidential, objective sound board for navigating complex leadership dilemmas and developing personalized strategies for well-being. Importantly, leaders should also encourage their teams to support one another, fostering a collective sense of responsibility for well-being.

Prioritizing mental health is not a luxury; it is a fundamental requirement for effective and enduring leadership. This involves proactively engaging in practices that safeguard mental well-being, rather than waiting until a crisis point is reached. This could include regular journaling to process thoughts and emotions, engaging in hobbies and activities that bring joy and a sense of accomplishment outside of work, and cultivating strong personal relationships that provide emotional sustenance. It also means being vigilant for the early signs of burnout in oneself, persistent fatigue, cynicism, a sense of inefficacy, or increased irritability and taking proactive steps to address these indicators. This might involve temporarily reducing workload where possible, delegating it more effectively, or taking a short break to recharge.

Moreover, leaders must actively model healthy behaviors. The adage "walk the talk" is particularly relevant here. If leaders are advocating for work-life balance, they must demonstrate it in their own lives. If they are encouraging open communication about well-being, they should be willing to share their own experiences (within appropriate professional boundaries) to normalize vulnerability. When leaders openly discuss their own strategies for managing stress, taking breaks, or setting boundaries, they create a ripple effect, signaling to their teams that these practices are not only permissible but encouraged. This modeling behavior is arguably one of the most powerful tools a leader has for shaping organizational culture. It communicates that taking care of oneself is a strength, not a weakness, and that sustained high performance is built on a foundation of personal resilience.

The organizational context also plays a crucial role in enabling leader self-care. Leaders must feel empowered by the broader organizational culture and leadership to prioritize their well-being. This means that the organizational structures and values must support, rather than undermine, these efforts. For example, if an organization implicitly rewards constant availability and overwork, even the most committed leader will struggle to maintain healthy boundaries. Therefore, a genuine commitment to a culture of care must extend to creating an environment where leaders feel psychologically safe to prioritize their own well-being without fear of negative repercussions. This might involve senior leadership openly endorsing and participating in wellness initiatives, ensuring that workloads are realistic, and providing access to resources that support mental and physical health.

In essence, self-care for leaders is not an act of selfishness; it is an act of profound responsibility. It is the foundation upon which sustainable, empathetic, and effective leadership is built. By consciously integrating stress management techniques, setting firm boundaries, actively seeking support, and prioritizing their mental health, leaders can not only prevent their own burnout but also create a more resilient, supportive, and ultimately, more caring environment for their entire teams. This proactive approach ensures that leaders can continue to guide their organizations with clarity, energy, and genuine compassion, fostering a culture of care that thrives because its leaders are themselves thriving. The ability to sustain one's own well-being is, therefore, the ultimate prerequisite for sustainably fostering the well-being of others, making self-care a non-negotiable imperative for true leadership. Leaders must view their personal capacity not as an inexhaustible resource, but as a vital asset that requires careful and consistent investment and maintenance, akin to any other critical business function. When leaders neglect this, the organization ultimately pays the price in reduced productivity, increased turnover, and a diminished capacity for innovation and growth, all stemming from a leadership that has inadvertently compromised its own ability to lead effectively by failing to lead itself with care.

The implementation of any significant cultural shift, particularly one as transformative as adopting "True Leadership" principles, is rarely a seamless process. It is far more common to encounter what is broadly termed "pushback" or "resistance to change." This is not necessarily an indictment of the principles themselves, nor an indicator of ill intent from those expressing them, but rather a natural human reaction to disruption, uncertainty, and the perceived threat to established norms. Understanding the multifaceted nature of this resistance is the first, crucial step in navigating it effectively and ensuring the sustained embedding of a culture of care.

The sources of pushback are as varied as the individuals within an organization. At its core, resistance often stems from a fundamental human inclination towards comfort and predictability. Individuals often favor what is familiar, as change inherently brings elements of uncertainty. This can manifest as quiet inertia, a subtle avoidance of new practices, or more overt questioning and opposition. One common vein of resistance is rooted in skepticism. This isn't necessarily a deliberate attempt to undermine the initiative, but rather a genuine doubt about its efficacy or feasibility. Skeptics might question whether these new principles can truly be implemented in this specific organizational context, given their unique history, industry pressures, or existing cultural norms. They might point to past initiatives that failed, or express concern that the proposed changes are too idealistic, lacking a practical roadmap for execution. This skepticism can be amplified if the communication around the change has been vague, lacking concrete examples or a clear vision of the desired future state.

Another significant source of resistance is the perceived threat of an increased workload or added complexity. Introducing new ways of leading and interacting, even those aimed at improving well-being, often requires learning new skills, adopting new communication protocols, and re-evaluating existing processes. For individuals already feeling stretched thin, the prospect of undertaking additional tasks or mental effort can be a significant deterrent. They might worry about the time required for training, the effort to adapt their existing routines, or the potential for mistakes as they navigate unfamiliar territory. This concern is particularly potent if the organization has a history of imposing new initiatives without adequate resourcing, training, or a realistic assessment of existing capacity. The fear isn't just about doing more work, but about doing more work *poorly* due to the learning curve or the lack of support.

Attachment to established ways of working, often referred to as "this is how we've always done it," is another powerful form of resistance. This mindset, while seemingly rooted in practicality, often masks a deeper emotional attachment to familiar routines, established power structures, and even a sense of identity tied to current practices. Employees with extended tenure often take pride in the processes they have contributed to developing and refining throughout their service. The suggestion that these methods need to change can feel like a personal criticism or a devaluation of their past contributions.

Furthermore, existing processes, even if suboptimal, provide a predictable framework. Changing them introduces uncertainty and requires individuals to develop new habits, which can be mentally taxing and disruptive to their established workflows and the comfort they derive from them.

Fear of the unknown is intrinsically linked to many of these sources of resistance. When individuals don't fully understand *why* a change is necessary, *what* it will entail, or *what the potential outcomes* might be, their natural inclination is to anticipate negative consequences. This can lead to a cascade of anxieties: Will I be able to adapt? Will this put me at a disadvantage? Will my role change in a way that makes me feel incompetent? Will this have an impact on my job security? These unspoken fears, if left unaddressed, can fester and become significant barriers to adoption.

Given these common sources of resistance, the approach to managing pushbacks must be deliberate, empathetic, and strategic. The first and perhaps most critical strategy is **empathetic communication**. This involves acknowledging and validating the concerns of those who are resistant, rather than dismissing them. It means actively listening, seeking to understand the underlying reasons for their apprehension, and reflecting that understanding back on them. Phrases like "I hear you saying that you're concerned about..." or "It sounds like you're worried about..." can go a long way in building trust and demonstrating that their perspective is valued. This empathetic approach doesn't necessarily mean agreeing with the resistance, but it signals respect and a willingness to engage in a genuine dialogue.

Transparency is equally vital. This means being upfront about the reasons for the change, the anticipated challenges, and the steps being taken to mitigate them. Instead of presenting the "True Leadership" principles as a fait accompli, leaders should articulate the vision, the benefits – both for the organization and for individuals – and the rationale behind the shift. This includes being honest about the potential for disruption and acknowledging that there will be a learning curve. When organizations are transparent about these aspects, they reduce the space for speculation and rumor, which often fuel fear and resistance. This transparency should extend to decision-making processes; where possible, involving individuals in shaping *how* the principles are implemented can significantly reduce feelings of powerlessness that often accompany externally imposed change.

Addressing concerns directly and proactively is another cornerstone of managing pushbacks. This involves anticipating the most common objections and preparing thoughtful, evidence-based responses. For instance, if the concern is about increased workloads, the response might involve clearly outlining the support structures, training resources, and any adjustments being made to manage the transition. It might also involve highlighting how the new principles, in the long run, can actually *reduce* certain types of workloads by improving efficiency, communication, and team cohesion. Demonstrating the tangible benefits through concrete examples is a powerful tool here. Rather than simply stating that "True Leadership fosters better teamwork," a leader might share a story of how a team, by adopting these principles, resolved a complex project bottleneck more effectively, saving significant time and resources. These "wins," even small ones, build credibility and provide tangible proof of concept.

Involving resistant individuals in the change process is a highly effective strategy for fostering understanding and building consensus. When people feel like they have a stake in the change, they are more likely to support it. This can take various forms. For those who are skeptical, inviting them to participate in pilot programs or task forces focused on implementing the principles can be beneficial. This gives them an opportunity to test the ideas, provide input on their application, and become advocates for the change based on their direct experience. For those concerned about workload, involving them in designing the implementation plan can help ensure that the process is realistic and manageable. This participatory approach also allows leaders to leverage the knowledge and experience of even the most resistant individuals, who may possess valuable insights into existing processes and potential pitfalls.

Furthermore, it is crucial to remember that resistance is not monolithic. Some resistance may be overt and vocal, while other forms can be more subtle and passive. Leaders need to be attuned to both. This might involve conducting surveys, holding focus groups, or simply engaging in regular one-on-one conversations to gauge sentiment. It's also important to distinguish between constructive feedback and obstructive resistance. Not all pushbacks are negative; often, they highlight genuine challenges or unintended consequences that, if addressed, can strengthen the change initiative. Leaders should create channels where feedback, even critical feedback, is welcomed and acted upon.

To illustrate, consider an organization that is transitioning to a more open communication style, a core tenet of True Leadership. Some team members, accustomed to formal, top-down directives, might express concern about "everyone having an opinion" or the perceived lack of clarity that can arise from broader discussions. A leader might address this by first acknowledging the value of established communication structures and the efficiency they sometimes offer. Then, they might explain how open dialogue, facilitated through regular team huddles or anonymous feedback channels, can surface potential problems early, foster innovation, and ensure that decisions are well-informed by diverse perspectives. To demonstrate this, they might showcase an instance where a team member's seemingly minor suggestion, raised in an open forum, prevented a costly error on a major project. This proactive framing and evidence-based illustration can disarm skepticism and highlight the benefits of the new approach.

Another scenario could involve a manager who is resistant to delegating tasks, fearing that it will increase their workload if they have to constantly supervise or correct their team. This resistance might stem from a belief that they can do the job faster and better themselves, or a fear that delegation indicates a lack of personal commitment. An empathetic response would involve acknowledging their dedication and desire for high-quality output. The leader might then explain that effective delegation is not about offloading work, but about developing team capacity, fostering engagement, and freeing up their own time for more strategic tasks. They could offer training on delegation skills, emphasize the importance of clear instructions and appropriate support, and perhaps suggest a phased approach where they start by delegating smaller, less critical tasks. Moreover, the leader could highlight how successful delegation leads to a more capable and empowered team, which in turn reduces the manager's overall burden and improves team performance, a tangible benefit.

The strategy of involving resistant individuals can be particularly effective when coupled with skill development. For example, if resistance stems from a fear of not knowing *how* to implement the new principles (e.g., how to have difficult conversations, how to provide constructive feedback without demotivating), offering targeted training and coaching can directly address this concern. This demonstrates a commitment to supporting individuals through the transition, rather than simply expecting them to adapt. It shifts the narrative from "you must change" to "we will help you change."

It is also important to identify and address the champions of resistance. Sometimes, pushbacks are not just a passive reaction but are actively promoted by individuals who may feel threatened by the change or who have a vested interest in maintaining the status quo. These individuals, if left unchecked, can have an outsized negative influence on the broader team. Leaders need to engage with these individuals directly, understand their concerns, and, where possible, try to bring them on board. However, if resistance persists and actively undermines the initiative, leaders may need to address the behavior more formally, reinforcing organizational expectations and consequences.

Chapter 15
Sustaining a Culture of Care

The long-term sustainability of a culture of care hinges on effectively navigating these challenges. It requires patience, persistence, and a willingness to adapt the implementation strategy based on feedback and observed outcomes. It also demands that leaders themselves embody the principles of True Leadership. If leaders consistently demonstrate empathy, transparency, and a commitment to addressing concerns, they create an environment where resistance is more likely to be expressed constructively and resolved effectively. Conversely, if leaders react defensively or dismissively to pushbacks, they will likely exacerbate the resistance and undermine the very culture of care they are trying to build.

Ultimately, managing pushbacks is not about eliminating all disagreement or ensuring universal enthusiasm. It is about fostering a process where concerns are heard, addressed thoughtfully, and where the rationale and benefits of the change become clear and compelling enough to foster buy-in and sustained adoption. By employing empathetic communication, transparency, direct concern resolution, and active involvement of those who are resistant, organizations can transform potential obstacles into opportunities for deeper understanding, stronger commitment, and a more robust and enduring culture of care. This proactive and people-centric approach to managing resistance is an integral part of leading authentically and sustainably. It acknowledges that change is a human journey, and that supporting individuals through that journey is as important as the destination itself. The success of integrating "True Leadership" principles, therefore, is as much about skillfully managing the inevitable human reactions to change as it is about the inherent merit of the principles themselves. This requires a consistent, observable commitment from leadership at all levels to not only championing the change but to actively engage with, understand, and address the varied concerns that arise, thereby building trust and fostering a shared commitment to the evolution of the organizational culture.

The journey toward a truly supportive and healthy workplace necessitates a direct confrontation with the insidious nature of mental health stigma. This pervasive issue, often rooted in misunderstanding, fear, and deeply ingrained societal biases, creates a silent barrier for many employees, preventing them from seeking the support they need and deserve. To cultivate a genuine culture of care, we must actively deconstruct this stigma, transforming our workplaces into environments where mental well-being is discussed with the same candor and acceptance as physical health. This is not merely about a passive absence of discrimination; it is about the proactive creation of an affirmative and inclusive atmosphere.

At the forefront of this deconstruction is the power of language. The words we use, both individually and collectively, carry immense weight in shaping perceptions and attitudes. Terms that trivialize or sensationalize mental health conditions, such as "crazy," "unstable," or "just a phase," can inadvertently reinforce negative stereotypes and discourage open dialogue. Similarly, employing euphemisms or speaking about mental health in hushed tones can perpetuate the idea that it is a taboo subject. Leaders and employees alike must become conscious of their linguistic choices, opting for person-first language and accurate, respectful terminology. Instead of saying "a schizophrenic," for instance, it is more appropriate and less stigmatizing to say, "a person with schizophrenia." This subtle but significant shift underscores that the condition is not the entirety of an individual's identity. Normalizing conversations about mental health requires embracing straightforward, empathetic, and non-judgmental language. It means discussing anxiety, depression, burnout, or stress with the same equanimity as one would discuss a sprained ankle, a common cold, or the need for a medical check-up. This requires a conscious effort to re-educate ourselves and our colleagues, fostering a vocabulary that is both accurate and compassionate.

The visible and vocal commitment of leadership is paramount in this endeavor. When leaders openly share their own experiences, where appropriate and comfortable, or champion mental health initiatives with genuine enthusiasm, they send a powerful signal throughout the organization. This could involve leaders participating in mental health awareness events, sharing resources, or simply initiating conversations about well-being during team meetings. For example, a CEO might begin a company-wide address by acknowledging the stresses of a demanding project and openly stating their own strategies for managing it, perhaps mentioning the importance of taking breaks or seeking support. This act of vulnerability and openness from the top can be incredibly effective in signaling that it is safe for others to do the same. It demystifies the concept of mental health challenges and demonstrates that seeking help is a sign of strength, not weakness. Leaders can also actively advocate for policies and programs that support mental well-being, ensuring that these initiatives are not just symbolic but are integrated into the operational fabric of the organization.

Furthermore, creating an environment where employees feel safe to discuss their mental health hinges on the implementation of inclusive and supportive policies. This extends beyond basic anti-discrimination clauses to encompass tangible provisions that actively promote mental wellness. This might include robust Employee Assistance Programs (EAPs) that are well-communicated, easily accessible, and have a broad range of services. It also involves reviewing existing policies to ensure they do not inadvertently penalize employees who need to take time off for mental health reasons. For instance, sick leave policies should explicitly include mental health conditions, and managers should be trained to handle requests for mental health-related leave with sensitivity and discretion. Flexible work arrangements, where feasible, can also be a crucial component of supporting employee mental well-being, allowing individuals to better manage stress and personal commitments. The key is to move from a reactive stance, where support is only offered when a crisis occurs, to a proactive one, where the organization actively fosters an environment conducive to good mental health for all.

Education and awareness campaigns play a critical role in dismantling stigma. Many misconceptions about mental health persist due to a lack of accurate information. Organizations can host workshops, webinars, or information sessions led by mental health professionals to educate employees about common mental health conditions, their signs and symptoms, and the available treatment options. These sessions should also focus on dispelling myths and stereotypes associated with mental illness. For example, a workshop could cover the difference between occasional stress and chronic anxiety, or explain that depression is a medical condition, not a character flaw. Providing resources such as informational pamphlets, online portals with relevant articles and helplines, and regular newsletters can also help to keep mental health at the forefront of employee awareness. The goal is to equip employees with the knowledge and understanding to recognize when they or a colleague might be struggling, and to feel confident in knowing how to respond supportively.

Normalizing help-seeking behavior requires a deliberate and consistent effort to create safe spaces for discussion. This can be achieved through various mechanisms, such as establishing peer support networks or mental health first aid training. Peer support groups, where employees can share experiences and offer mutual encouragement, can be incredibly powerful in breaking down feelings of isolation. Mental Health First Aiders, trained individuals within the organization who can provide initial support and guidance to those experiencing mental health difficulties, act as accessible points of contact.

The availability of these resources, and clear communication about their existence and purpose, signals to employees that the organization prioritizes their mental well-being. It is also important to ensure that these support systems are well-integrated and that there are clear pathways for escalation to professional help when needed.

Moreover, actively fostering a culture of psychological safety is fundamental. Psychological safety is the belief that one will not be punished or humiliated for speaking up with ideas, questions, concerns, or mistakes. In the context of mental health, this means creating an environment where employees feel comfortable disclosing mental health challenges or seeking support without fear of negative repercussions, such as judgment, career stagnation, or social exclusion. This is built through consistent leadership behaviors that demonstrate respect, empathy, and a willingness to listen. When leaders model vulnerability and actively solicit feedback, even critical feedback, they create a foundation of trust upon which psychological safety can flourish. Regular check-ins by managers, focused not just on task completion but on the overall well-being of their team members, can also contribute significantly to this sense of safety. These check-ins should be opportunities for genuine connection, where employees feel heard and supported.

The impact of unchecked mental health stigma can be profound, leading to decreased productivity, increased absenteeism, higher turnover rates, and a general erosion of morale. Conversely, actively deconstructing stigma and prioritizing mental well-being yields significant organizational benefits. Employees who feel supported in their mental health are more likely to be engaged, innovative, and loyal. They are also more likely to contribute positively to team dynamics and the overall organizational culture. This is not just a matter of social responsibility; it is a strategic imperative for any organization aiming to thrive in today's complex and demanding world.

To further illustrate the practical application of these strategies, consider the role of team meetings. Instead of starting every meeting with a purely task-oriented agenda, a leader might begin with a brief "well-being check-in." This could be as simple as asking each team member to share the one thing they are doing to manage their stress or one positive aspect of their week. This sets a tone that acknowledges the human element of work and normalizes discussions about personal well-being. Another example is the implementation of a "mental health champion" program, where volunteer employees receive specialized training and act as advocates within their departments, disseminating information and providing informal support. These champions can help to designate conversations by being visible role models and approachable resources.

The integration of mental health into performance management discussions can also be a powerful tool, provided it is handled with sensitivity and a focus on support. Instead of viewing mental health as a separate, siloed issue, it can be discussed as a factor that impacts overall performance and engagement. For instance, a manager might observe a decline in an employee's output or engagement and, during a one-on-one, gently inquire about their well-being, offering support or suggesting resources if the employee chooses to disclose any challenges. This approach should always be framed around support and development, not as a disciplinary measure. It requires managers to be trained in having these sensitive conversations and to understand the boundaries and ethical considerations involved.

The role of storytelling in combating stigma cannot be overstated. Sharing personal narratives, whether through internal communication channels, company events, or dedicated platforms, can humanize mental health challenges and create powerful connections. When individuals hear stories from colleagues who have navigated similar difficulties and emerged stronger, it can be incredibly validating and empowering. These stories serve as a testament to resilience and the effectiveness of seeking help. It is crucial, however, that such storytelling is voluntary and that individuals are empowered to share their experiences in a way that feels safe and authentic, with appropriate support mechanisms in place. The organization must ensure that there is no implicit or explicit pressure to share personal health information.

Furthermore, an organization's external reputation and brand can also be influenced by its commitment to mental well-being. In an era where employee well-being is increasingly valued by job seekers, companies that demonstrate a genuine commitment to mental health are more attractive to top talent. Conversely, organizations perceived as having a toxic culture or failing to support their employees' mental health will struggle to recruit and retain the best people. This external perception reinforces the internal imperative to actively deconstruct mental health stigma.

The challenge of deconstructing mental health stigma is an ongoing process, not a one-time fix. It requires sustained effort, continuous learning, and a willingness to adapt strategies as organizational needs and societal understanding evolve. It involves embedding mental health support and awareness into the very DNA of the organization, making it an intrinsic part of the culture rather than an add-on program. Leaders must consistently model the behaviors they wish to see, creating a ripple effect that permeates all levels of the organization. By prioritizing open communication, providing accessible resources, implementing supportive policies, and fostering an environment of psychological safety, organizations can effectively dismantle the barriers of stigma and create workplaces where every employee feels valued, respected, and empowered to thrive, both personally and professionally. This transformation is not just about managing mental health; it's about building a fundamentally healthier, more resilient, and more human-centric organization. The investment in deconstructing mental health stigma is an investment in the well-being of people, the productivity of teams, and the long-term success of the enterprise. It is a testament to the core principles of true leadership, where care is not just a value but a lived practice.

The emphasis on language extends to the way we frame workplace stressors. Instead of describing demanding projects as inherently "stressful" in a way that suggests unavoidable suffering, leaders can frame them as "challenging" and emphasize the organizational support systems in place to manage these challenges. This subtle shift in language can help to reframe the experience of pressure from something debilitating to something surmountable with the right approach and support. For instance, when a significant project deadline looms, a leader might communicate by saying, "This is a demanding period, and we're all feeling the intensity. Let's ensure we're utilizing our flexible work options and remembering to take short breaks to recharge. If anyone feels overwhelmed, please reach out to your manager or HR; we have resources available." This approach acknowledges the reality of the situation while actively promoting coping mechanisms and available support.

Moreover, the practice of providing regular, constructive feedback is a crucial avenue for addressing potential mental health challenges subtly and supportively. When managers are trained to observe changes in an employee's work patterns, such as decreased attention to detail, missed deadlines, or social withdrawal, they can use the feedback process as an opportunity to inquire about their overall well-being. This isn't about diagnosing or probing into personal matters but about opening a door for conversation. A manager might say, "I've noticed that [specific observation], and I want to ensure you have the support you need. How are things going generally? Is there anything affecting your ability to perform at your best?" This type of feedback, delivered with genuine care and without judgment, can encourage employees to share if they are comfortable, or at least feel acknowledged and supported. The crucial element here is that the manager is prepared to listen and to guide the employee towards appropriate resources if they choose to disclose any difficulties. This proactive approach, embedded in regular performance conversations, can be far more effective than waiting for a crisis to erupt.

The concept of normalizing help-seeking also involves destigmatizing the use of mental health days or time off for mental health reasons. Just as an employee would readily take a sick day for the flu, they should feel equally comfortable taking a "mental health day" when they are experiencing burnout or significant emotional distress. This requires explicit communication from leadership and a clear, supportive policy that reinforces this parity. When organizations champion the idea that mental health is a component of overall health, taking time to rest and recover from mental fatigue becomes as accepted as taking time to recover from physical illness. This can be reinforced through internal communications, manager training, and by leaders themselves openly utilizing and advocating for such practices. When a leader openly takes a day off to "recharge" and returns refreshed, it normalizes the behavior for the entire organization.

Considering mental health in broader organizational well-being initiatives is also vital. This means that discussions about mental health should not be isolated events but should be woven into broader conversations about physical health, stress management, work-life balance, and employee engagement. By adopting a holistic approach, organizations can demonstrate that mental well-being is an integral part of overall health and that it is valued and supported in a comprehensive manner. This might involve offering workshops on mindfulness and stress reduction, promoting healthy lifestyle choices, and ensuring that workplace environments are designed to promote well-being. When mental health is part of this broader tapestry, it becomes less of a distinct, potentially stigmatized topic and more of an accepted aspect of everyday life and work.

Finally, the continuous evaluation and refinement of mental health strategies are essential. What works for one organization or team might not work for another, and the needs of employees can evolve over time. Regularly soliciting feedback from employees through surveys, focus groups, or anonymous feedback channels can help identify areas for improvement and ensure that mental health initiatives remain relevant and effective. This iterative process of listening, adapting, and improving is a hallmark of a truly committed and responsive organization. By actively engaging employees in the development and refinement of these strategies, organizations can foster a sense of ownership and ensure that the culture of care is not only established but is also sustainable and impactful for everyone.

Embedding care into core leadership functions and performance management is not merely an add-on program; it's about fundamentally redesigning how we lead and how we measure success. This involves a strategic and intentional integration of well-being principles into every facet of the employee lifecycle, from the initial attraction of talent to their ongoing development and evaluation. When care is woven into the fabric of these core processes, it signals a deep-seated commitment that permeates the entire organizational culture, making supportive leadership not just a desirable trait but an expected and rewarded one.

The journey begins with recruitment and onboarding. The language used in job descriptions and during interviews can set the tone. Instead of solely focusing on technical skills and past achievements, organizations can incorporate language that highlights their commitment to employee well-being, a supportive work environment, and a culture of care. For example, a job post might include a statement about valuing work-life balance, fostering psychological safety, or supporting continuous learning and personal growth. During interviews, questions can be designed to assess a candidate's understanding of and commitment to empathetic leadership and team support. This could involve behavioral questions such as, "Describe a time you supported a team member through a challenging personal or professional situation," or "How do you foster a sense of belonging within a team?" Assessing these qualities early ensures that new hires are not only skilled but also aligned with the organization's values of care. The onboarding process is another critical touchpoint. Beyond the standard paperwork and introductions to company policies, onboarding should actively introduce new employees to the organization's culture of care. This includes clearly communicating available mental health resources, introducing them to mental health champions or support networks, and explaining the organization's stance on psychological safety and well-being. A well-designed onboarding program can proactively equip new employees with the knowledge and confidence to seek support when needed and to contribute to a positive and caring environment from day one. Sharing stories of how care is practiced within the organization, perhaps through testimonials from existing employees or leaders, can further solidify this message.

Talent development and employee growth must also be viewed through the lens of care. Leaders are instrumental in nurturing the potential of their teams, and this nurturing extends beyond technical skill development to encompass the holistic well-being of their people. When organizations invest in leadership development programs, they should explicitly include modules on emotional intelligence, empathetic communication, stress management for themselves and their teams, and the ability to foster psychological safety. Training managers to conduct sensitive and supportive one-on-one meetings is paramount. These meetings should be structured not just for performance updates but as opportunities to connect, understand individual needs, and identify any potential barriers to well-being. Managers should be equipped with the skills to recognize early signs of distress or burnout and to offer appropriate support or direct employees to relevant resources. This proactive approach to development ensures that leaders are not only effective in driving results but also in cultivating a healthy and supportive environment for their teams. Furthermore, career development discussions should acknowledge the role of well-being in sustained performance and career longevity. Encouraging employees to set realistic goals, manage their workloads effectively, and prioritize their health is a sign of true leadership care.

Performance management systems are often seen as purely metrics-driven, but they can and should be transformed to reflect a commitment to care. This involves broadening the definition of performance to include aspects like collaboration, contribution to team morale, and demonstration of company values, including empathy and support for colleagues. When performance reviews are conducted, they should provide a balanced perspective that considers not only task completion and objective achievements but also how an individual contributes to a positive and supportive work environment. Leaders should be trained to provide feedback that is constructive, specific, and delivered with empathy, focusing on growth and development rather than solely on identifying shortcomings. For instance, instead of simply stating that an employee missed a deadline, a manager might explore the underlying reasons, such as workload management challenges or personal stressors, and offer support or resources to help the employee succeed in the future.

Integrating well-being into performance metrics means that supportive behaviors are recognized and rewarded. This could manifest in various ways. For example, a performance appraisal might include a section on "team contribution" or "values demonstration," where an employee's efforts in supporting colleagues, fostering a positive team dynamic, or championing well-being initiatives are explicitly acknowledged and contribute to their overall evaluation. This recognition can be further reinforced through incentive programs, bonuses, or promotion criteria that explicitly value and reward these supportive leadership qualities. When individuals see that demonstrating care and empathy has tangible benefits for their career progression, it reinforces the importance of these behaviors throughout the organization. Conversely, performance management systems should also address behaviors that undermine a culture of care. This includes identifying and addressing instances of poor leadership, disrespect, or a lack of support for team members, with clear pathways for intervention and development.

The feedback mechanisms within performance management are also crucial for embedding care. Encouraging upward feedback, where employees can provide feedback to their managers and leaders on their leadership style and supportiveness, is essential. This creates a two-way accountability system that ensures leaders are living up to the organization's commitment to care. Using and responding to feedback channels shows the organization values employees and strives to improve leadership. Anonymous feedback options can be particularly effective in encouraging honest and candid input, allowing employees to share their experiences without fear of reprisal.

The role of leaders in championing these integrated processes is paramount. They must not only understand the importance of embedding care into leadership functions and performance management but also actively model these behaviors. This means demonstrating empathy in their interactions, prioritizing the well-being of their teams, and openly supporting the organization's mental health initiatives. When leaders actively participate in training, advocate for supportive policies, and consistently demonstrate caring behaviors, they set a powerful example for others to follow. This visible commitment from the top creates a ripple effect, encouraging other managers and employees to adopt similar practices.

Furthermore, organizations can implement formal recognition programs that specifically acknowledge leaders and employees who exemplify a culture of care. This could involve "care awards," "teamwork recognition," or shout-outs in company communications for individuals who have gone above and beyond to support their colleagues. These forms of recognition not only celebrate positive behaviors but also serve as powerful educational tools, highlighting what constitutes caring leadership and employee conduct within the organization. By consistently reinforcing that care is a valued and rewarded aspect of performance, organizations can solidify their position as a core leadership function and an integral part of how success is defined and measured. This systemic approach ensures that the commitment to well-being is not a fleeting initiative but a deeply ingrained aspect of the organizational DNA, making true leadership synonymous with genuine care.

Integrating care into workplace operations also requires reevaluating team structures and the way tasks are assigned. Leaders who are attuned to well-being understand the importance of manageable workloads, realistic deadlines, and equitable distribution of tasks. This means moving beyond simply assigning tasks to the most capable individuals and instead considering factors such as individual capacity, potential for burnout, and the need for development opportunities. Managers equipped with an understanding of their team members' strengths, challenges, and personal circumstances can make more informed decisions about task allocation, ensuring that no single individual is consistently overburdened. This proactive approach to workload management is a fundamental act of care, demonstrating that the organization values the health and sustainability of its workforce.

Moreover, the concept of "accountability for care" needs to be clearly defined and communicated at all levels. This means that leaders are not only accountable for achieving business objectives but also for fostering a supportive and healthy work environment. Performance metrics for leaders should reflect their success in building engaged teams, promoting well-being, and demonstrating empathetic leadership. This might involve incorporating feedback from direct reports into their performance evaluations, or setting specific goals related to employee engagement scores, retention rates, or participation in well-being programs. When leaders are held accountable for these aspects of their role, it elevates the importance of care from personal preference to professional responsibility.

The communication of these integrated practices is equally vital. Organizations must continuously communicate their commitment to care and well-being, ensuring that employees understand how these principles are embedded in leadership functions and performance management. Internal communications, town hall meetings, and leadership addresses can all be used to reinforce these messages, sharing success stories, highlighting supportive behaviors, and reiterating the organization's values. This consistent communication helps to build trust and reinforces the message that well-being is a genuine priority, not just a platitude. Transparency about how performance is assessed and how supportive behaviors are recognized is also crucial. Employees need to understand the criteria used in performance reviews and the pathways for career advancement, ensuring that these processes are perceived as fair and equitable. That care is indeed a valued component of success.

Furthermore, the concept of "learning from failure" in the context of care is also important. Leaders should be encouraged to view mistakes or instances where support was not adequately provided as learning opportunities, rather than as failures that lead to punishment. This requires a culture that embraces psychological safety, where individuals feel comfortable admitting when they have made mistakes or fallen short, and where the focus is on learning and improving for the future. Managers who are open to receiving feedback about their own leadership effectiveness, and who are willing to adapt their approach based on that feedback, are invaluable in fostering a truly caring culture. This continuous learning and adaptation cycle ensures that the organization's approach to care remains relevant and effective.

The integration of care into performance management also extends to how feedback is delivered regarding employee well-being. If an employee's performance is declining, a manager's approach should be to explore potential contributing factors, including stressors or challenges affecting their well-being, rather than solely focusing on the performance deficit. This requires training managers to have empathetic conversations, to listen actively, and to guide employees towards available resources, such as the Employee Assistance Program (EAP), mental health support services, or flexible work arrangements. The objective is to support the employee in overcoming obstacles and returning to their optimal performance level, recognizing that well-being and performance are intrinsically linked. This approach shifts the performance conversation from one of judgment to one of support and collaboration.

In essence, embedding care into core leadership functions and performance management is about creating a virtuous cycle. By prioritizing well-being in recruitment and onboarding, investing in leaders' ability to support their teams, integrating caring behaviors into performance evaluations, and consistently recognizing and rewarding these attributes, organizations foster an environment where both individuals and the organization can thrive. This systemic approach ensures that care is not an afterthought but a fundamental component of effective leadership and a key driver of sustainable success. It transforms the workplace into a place where people feel valued, supported, and empowered to do their best work, knowing that their well-being is a genuine organizational priority. This is the essence of true leadership, where the success of the enterprise is built upon the foundation of its people's health and happiness.

The journey toward embedding True Leadership and fostering a culture of care is not a destination, but an ongoing evolution. To ensure that the deep-seated commitment to employee well-being and empathetic leadership becomes a resilient, enduring characteristic of the organization, a deliberate and sustained strategy is paramount. This involves moving beyond initial implementation and establishing robust systems that promote continuous learning, adaptation, and reinforcement of these vital principles. The aim is to create a self-sustaining ecosystem where care is not a program, but the very operating system of the business, ensuring long-term organizational health and the flourishing of every individual within it.

A cornerstone of sustaining this momentum lies in the commitment to perpetual learning and development for leaders at all levels. While initial training sessions are crucial for introducing concepts of empathetic leadership, emotional intelligence, and psychological safety, these skills require ongoing refinement and reinforcement. Organizations must therefore invest in continuous learning pathways that address emerging challenges and evolving best practices in well-being. This might include advanced workshops on trauma-informed leadership, strategies for supporting diverse employee needs, or techniques for fostering resilience in the face of organizational change. Furthermore, creating opportunities for leaders to share their experiences, challenges, and successes in practicing empathetic leadership can foster a collaborative learning environment. Peer-to-peer learning, facilitated through mentorship programs or regular leader forums, allows for the sharing of practical insights and the collective development of solutions. Such forums can also serve as a space to discuss difficult scenarios and collectively brainstorm approaches that align with the organization's values of care, ensuring that leaders are equipped to navigate complex situations with empathy and effectiveness.

Beyond individual leader development, a critical element of sustainability involves the regular and systematic review of organizational policies and practices through the lens of care. What was considered best practice yesterday may need to be re-evaluated in light of new understanding or changing employee needs. This necessitates establishing a cadence for reviewing HR policies, performance management frameworks, and operational guidelines to ensure they consistently reflect and support a culture of care. For instance, policies related to flexible work arrangements, leave entitlements, or conflict resolution should be periodically assessed to determine their effectiveness in promoting employee well-being and fairness. This review process should not be a top-down exercise but should actively involve input from employees and teams at various levels. Surveys, focus groups, and employee resource groups can provide invaluable feedback on how existing policies are experienced in practice and identify areas where adjustments are needed. This participatory approach ensures that policies remain relevant and genuinely supportive of the workforce.

Celebrating successes, both big and small, is another vital component in sustaining a culture of care. Recognizing and acknowledging instances where leaders and employees have demonstrated exemplary empathetic behavior or contributed to a positive and supportive work environment reinforces the value placed on these actions. This can take many forms, from formal awards and public recognition in company-wide communications to informal shout-outs in team meetings or personalized messages from senior leadership. The key is to make these acknowledgments authentic and visible, demonstrating that the organization actively observes and appreciates efforts that uphold its values. When employees see that their commitment to care is noticed and celebrated, it not only boosts morale but also encourages others to emulate these positive behaviors, creating a virtuous cycle of caring actions. These celebrations serve as tangible evidence that the organization's commitment to well-being is not merely rhetoric but a lived reality.

Fostering a feedback-rich environment is fundamental to ensuring the long-term resilience and adaptability of a caring culture. This involves creating multiple, accessible, and safe channels for employees to provide feedback on their experiences, including their perceptions of leadership support, workload balance, and the overall work environment. Encouraging upward feedback, where employees can share their perspectives with their managers and leaders without fear, is crucial. This can be facilitated through anonymous survey tools, suggestion boxes, or dedicated feedback sessions. Critically, it is not enough to simply solicit feedback; organizations must demonstrate that this feedback is heard, valued, and acted upon. Transparent communication about how feedback is being used to inform policy changes, leadership development initiatives, or operational adjustments builds trust and reinforces the organizational commitment to continuous improvement. When employees see that their voices are instrumental in shaping their workplace, they are more likely to remain engaged and invested in the collective effort to foster a caring culture. This feedback loop is the organizational immune system, helping to identify and address potential issues before they escalate and ensuring that the culture of care remains robust and responsive to the evolving needs of its people.

Moreover, embedding a long-term perspective on care requires the establishment of clear accountability mechanisms. Leaders at all levels must understand that their responsibility extends beyond operational targets to include the well-being and development of their teams. This accountability can be integrated into performance reviews, leadership development programs, and succession planning processes. For example, a leader's effectiveness could be evaluated not only on their team's productivity but also on metrics related to employee engagement, retention, psychological safety, and the team's overall well-being. By making care a tangible aspect of leadership performance, organizations signal that it is a non-negotiable component of effective leadership. This ensures that the focus on employee well-being is not contingent on individual leader discretion but is a consistent expectation across the organization.

The evolution of a resilient culture of care also necessitates an ongoing dialogue about the organization's values and how they translate into everyday practices. Regular communication from senior leadership, reinforcing commitment to True Leadership and well-being, is essential. This can be achieved through town hall meetings, internal newsletters, and candid conversations that address both achievements and ongoing challenges. Transparency about the organization's efforts to support employee well-being, including sharing data on key indicators and outlining future plans, fosters a sense of shared purpose and collective ownership of the culture. When employees feel informed and involved in the ongoing journey of cultivating care, they become more invested in its success and more likely to contribute to its perpetuation. This continuous communication acts as a constant reminder of the organization's core commitments and its dedication to fostering a truly supportive and healthy workplace.

Furthermore, cultivating resilience means preparing for and proactively addressing potential disruptions or stressors that might impact employee well-being. This could involve developing crisis communication protocols, establishing clear support pathways during times of significant organizational change or external challenges, and ensuring that leaders are equipped to guide their teams through uncertainty with empathy and transparency. A resilient culture of care is one that not only provides support during good times but also demonstrates unwavering commitment and resilience during difficult periods. This proactive approach to anticipating and managing challenges builds trust. It strengthens the organizational fabric, ensuring that the focus on care remains a guiding principle even in the face of adversity.

Embedding care within the core values of an organization involves considering not only employee well-being but also the wider ecosystem. This might involve fostering partnerships with external mental health providers, engaging in community initiatives that promote well-being, or advocating for policies that support mental health in the wider society. By extending its commitment to care beyond its own employees, the organization reinforces its values and contributes to a more positive societal impact. This outward-looking approach not only strengthens the organization's reputation but also cultivates a deeper sense of purpose and meaning for its employees, further embedding the culture of care into its identity.

Finally, the long-term sustainability of a culture of care hinges on its ability to adapt and evolve. The needs and expectations of the workforce are not static; they change with societal trends, technological advancements, and the personal journeys of individuals. Therefore, organizations must remain agile and open to continuous learning and improvement. This means actively monitoring employee sentiment, staying abreast of research in organizational well-being, and being willing to experiment with new approaches. By fostering a mindset of perpetual innovation and adaptation, organizations can ensure that their commitment to True Leadership and a culture of care remains relevant, effective, and deeply ingrained for years to come, fostering a workplace where individuals not only survive but truly thrive. This ongoing commitment to growth and adaptation is the ultimate testament to the enduring power of care.

Back Matter

This book is the culmination of years of practical application, research, and, most importantly, invaluable conversations with countless leaders and employees who have bravely shared their experiences. I am deeply grateful to all those who have contributed their insights, often in vulnerable moments, shaping the understanding presented within these pages. My sincere thanks go to the organizations that have opened their doors, allowing for the implementation and refinement of the principles of True Leadership and a culture of care. Special recognition is due to my mentors and colleagues, whose guidance and challenging questions have been instrumental in my own development. Finally, I extend my profound gratitude to my family and friends for their unwavering support and patience throughout this endeavor.

The appendix serves as a practical toolkit for organizations and leaders committed to embedding and sustaining a culture of care. It includes actionable resources designed to complement the strategies discussed throughout the book. Within this section, you will find:

Assessment Tools: Sample questionnaires and frameworks for evaluating current organizational culture, leadership empathy, and employee well-being, allowing for baseline measurement and progress tracking.

Workshop Outlines: Detailed session plans for key workshops on topics such as building psychological safety, developing empathetic communication, and fostering resilience. These include learning objectives, activities, and discussion prompts.

Policy Review Checklists: Comprehensive checklists to guide the review and revision of HR policies, performance management systems, and operational guidelines, ensuring alignment with the principles of care.

Communication Templates: Examples of internal communications for reinforcing the culture of care, celebrating successes, and transparently sharing feedback outcomes.

Recommended Reading and Resources: A curated list of further academic research, books, and relevant organizations that offer deeper dives into leadership, organizational psychology, and workplace well-being.

Case Study Summaries: Brief overviews of organizational initiatives that have successfully implemented the concepts discussed, highlighting key strategies and outcomes.

This glossary defines key terms and concepts used throughout the book, ensuring clarity and a shared understanding of the terminology central to True Leadership and fostering a culture of care.

Authentic Leadership: A leadership style characterized by self-awareness, transparency, and a strong internal moral compass, leading with integrity and genuine intention.

Care as an Operating System: The integration of care principles into the fundamental structures, processes, and daily operations of an organization, making it an inherent part of how business is conducted, rather than a separate initiative.

Culture of Care: An organizational environment where the well-being, dignity, and development of every individual are prioritized, respected, and actively supported through daily actions, policies, and leadership behaviors.

Empathetic Leadership: The ability of leaders to understand and share the feelings of others, using this understanding to inform their decisions, interactions, and support for their teams.

Emotional Intelligence (EI): The capacity to be aware of, control, and express one's emotions, and to handle interpersonal relationships judiciously and empathetically.

Feedback-Rich Environment: A workplace where open, honest, and constructive feedback is regularly exchanged between individuals at all levels, delivered and received with respect and a commitment to growth.

Psychological Safety: A shared belief held by members of a team that the team is safe for interpersonal risk-taking; that is, people feel comfortable being themselves, speaking up with ideas, questions, concerns, or mistakes without fear of negative consequences.

Resilience (Organizational): The capacity of an organization to anticipate, prepare for, respond to, and recover from disruptions, maintaining its core functions and adapting effectively to change while prioritizing the well-being of its people.

Sustained Momentum: The ongoing and consistent application of strategies and practices that reinforce a culture of care, ensuring its longevity and adaptability beyond initial implementation phases.

True Leadership: A holistic approach to leadership that integrates effectiveness with empathy, integrity, and a profound commitment to the well-being and growth of individuals and the organization as a whole.

The insights and strategies presented in this book are grounded in established research and best practices within organizational psychology, leadership development, and human resources. The following represent a selection of the foundational works and influential studies that have informed this publication. Full academic citations are available upon request, and specific works are referenced throughout the text where appropriate to acknowledge their direct contribution to the concepts discussed.

Bibliography

Adams, J. (2019). The Resilience Factor: How to Thrive in the Face of Adversity.

Argyris, C., & Schön, D. A. (1978). Organizational Learning: A Theory of Action Perspective.

Bradberry, T., & Greaves, J. (2009). Emotional Intelligence 2.0.

Cameron, K. S., & Quinn, R. E. (2011). Diagnosing and Changing Organizational Culture: Based on the Competing Values Framework.

Edmonson, A. C. (1999). Psychological Safety and Learning Behavior in Work Teams. Administrative Science Quarterly, 44(2), 350–383.

Goleman, D. (1995). Emotional Intelligence: Why It Can Matter More Than IQ.

Kahn, W. M. (1990). Psychological Conditions of Personal Engagement and Disengagement at Work. Academy of Management Journal, 33(4), 704–727.

Lencioni, P. M. (2002). The Five Dysfunctions of a Team: A Leadership Fable.

Maslow, A. H. (1943). A theory of human motivation. Psychological Review, 50(4), 370–396.

Nye, J. S. (2004). Soft Power: The Means to Success in World Politics.

Sinek, S. (2011). Start With Why: How Great Leaders Inspire Everyone to Take Action.

Uhl-Bien, M. (2006). Relational Leadership Theory: Exploring the Social Processes of Leadership and Organizing. The Leadership Quarterly, 17(6), 617–639.

About the Author

Mackens Salomon is a leadership consultant, organizational strategist, and researcher with more than two decades of experience cultivating high-performing, human-centered workplace cultures. Throughout his career, he has supported government agencies, nonprofit organizations, and private-sector companies in implementing large-scale wellbeing and mental health initiatives designed to strengthen engagement, resilience, and long-term organizational health. Recognized for his practical insights and empathetic leadership approach, Salomon specializes in helping leaders navigate complex workplace challenges while building systems that support sustainable performance. His work focuses on reducing burnout, enhancing psychological safety, and fostering environments where employees feel valued, supported, and motivated to excel.

This book is the culmination of years of hands-on practice, research, and a deep commitment to a simple truth: People thrive when supported and organizations thrive when people do.

Beyond his professional life, Salomon enjoys reading, watching leadership, socioeconomic development, and healthcare-focused programs, bowling, and spending meaningful time with his family.

Made in the USA
Coppell, TX
08 June 2026

79203192R00144